Tennis

Strokes and tactics
to improve your game

John Littleford & Andrew Magrath

Note
Whilst every effort has been made to
ensure that the content of this book is as
technically accurate and as sound as
possible, neither the authors nor the
publishers can accept responsibility for
any injury or loss sustained as a result of
the use of this material.

A QUARTO BOOK

Published in 2010 by
A&C Black Publishers
36 Soho Square
London W1D 3QY
www.acblack.com

ISBN: 978 14081 1558 9

Conceived, designed, and produced by
Quarto Publishing plc
The Old Brewery
6 Blundell Street
London
N7 9BH

QUAR.TEBK

Senior editor: Katie Hallam
Copy editor: Claire Waite-Brown
Art director: Caroline Guest
Designer: Tania Devonshire-Jones
Design assistant: Saffron Stocker
Picture research: Sarah Bell
Photographer: Simon Pask
Creative director: Moira Clinch
Publisher: Paul Carslake

Colour separation by PICA Digital Pte Ltd,
Singapore
Printed in China by 1010 Printing
International Ltd.

contents

Introduction   6
About this book   7

The strokes   8

First steps   10
Get a grip   12
Forehand topspin   16
Two-handed topspin backhand   24
One-handed topspin backhand   32
One-handed slice backhand   38
One-handed backhand drop shot   45
Sidespin slice serve   46
Topslice/topspin serve   54
Slice forehand   62
Forehand drop shot   69
High forehand volley   70
Forehand drop volley   74
Low forehand volley   76
Forehand half volley   80
Medium backhand volley   82
Backhand drop volley   86
Low backhand volley   88
Backhand half volley   92
Returns of serve   94
Forehand topspin lob   100
Backhand topspin lob   108
Forehand smash   114
Backhand smash   120
Forehand drive volley   126
One-handed backhand drive volley   132
Two-handed backhand drive volley   136

Learning the ropes   140

Getting started   142
Scoring   144
Serving and rallying rules   146
Court etiquette   148

Tactics   150

Tactical serving   152
Tactical returning   154
Tactical first strikes   156
Cross court and down the line   158
Rallying tactics   160
20 steps to the right mindset   162
Doubles tactics and formations   164
The returning player   170

Glossary   172
Index   174
Credits   176

Introduction

Tennis is a fabulous game that seems to bring the best out of people, whatever their background or wherever they come from.

The first time, as toddlers, that our parents threw us a tennis ball, our passion for the sport was born, and watching Wimbledon on television from an early age further fuelled our enthusiasm. Witnessing McEnroe's epic encounters with Bjorg, and later the athletic antics of Boris Becker, made many tennis kids dive across the court to reach a volley at no thought of injury to themselves, even those who played on tarmac.

Teaching is in our blood, since we both have parents who taught, and we count ourselves very fortunate to be able to teach others this wonderful sport that we both love. It gives us a real buzz to see the satisfied faces of people enjoying the skills we have imparted. That is why we are so passionate about the simple system we have described in this book. If you follow it thoroughly you will literally be playing tennis in minutes, and the tennis world will be yours.

About this book

The strokes

Each shot is broken down into stages

Central aerial shots show the player's stance and racket position

The position of the ball is marked where relevant for a fuller understanding of the shot in action

The integral change in grip is enhanced for added detail

Additional notes explain the natural movements of the player

Directional arrows indicate the swing of the racket

Accurate photography covers all the angles

Regular "mantras" remind you of the key concepts to remember as you play

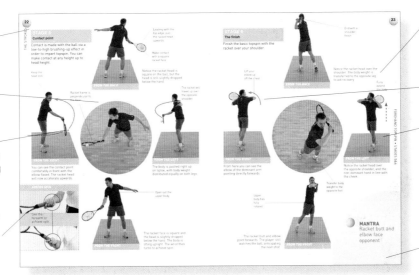

Key to strokes

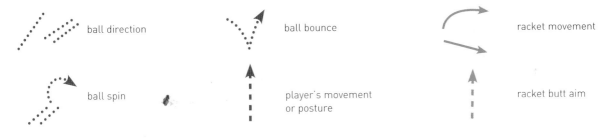

ball direction

ball bounce

racket movement

ball spin

player's movement or posture

racket butt aim

Learning the ropes/Tactics

The back section rounds up the other important elements of the game.

Key elements of the game are examined in detail

Added notes provide useful snippets of information

Simple diagrams illustrate the points discussed

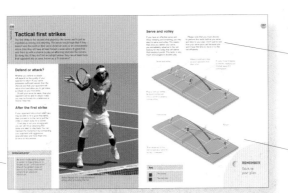

the strokes

You may have heard that tennis is a complicated sport to learn, when this simply is not the case — especially now that you have this book to guide you through. The only thing complicated about tennis is the way it is sometimes taught.

Novak Djokovic of Serbia reaches for a wide forehand return during the French Open.

First steps

Many coaches launch into teaching complete beginners techniques that are way beyond their grasp. Many beginners feel clumsy at first, even just holding a racket, yet coaches expect them to perform the perfect swing while remaining fairly static. Not only is this approach complicated and awkward, it is, for the most part, completely boring. The student is not rallying or playing points, basically doing none of the things that make tennis exciting.

So what's the answer? The techniques described on the following pages set the novice tennis player on a positive road to success, ensuring that you feel comfortable with the ball and the strokes before you even pick up a racket, and all the while learning the rules and tactics of the game.

Learn with the hands first

A good way to begin learning to play tennis is to do so without a racket. This may start with a simple game of throw and catch, an exercise that teaches how to move naturally to the ball. Further exercises without the racket allow you to learn about the coordination of how to receive the ball, and can help you get to grips with the rules of tennis by introducing points.

Exercises include learning how to push the ball with the hands but without swinging the arms. You can also rally over the net with a partner just by pushing the ball to each other. Your feel for the ball will start to develop, but more importantly you will have fun.

As you progress through the shots depicted in this book, including the forehand topspin, backhand, serve and so on, do so with the hands first, to enhance your feel for the ball. Even just by using the hands you will be able to spin the ball as it would when struck with the racket; the only difference is that the racket will impart more power.

Playing games with a partner using just your hands allows you to learn basic tennis tactics in order to win.

"Pushing and posing": Push the ball up with the hand...

...and move the hand over the shoulder, elbow pointing forwards.

Repeat with a racket: hold the racket at the throat, imagining the racket head is your hand.

Pull the racket up and over the shoulder, racket butt pointing forwards.

Tracking the ball

You now need to learn to focus on what is happening in front of you, rather than what is going on behind you. You do this by tracking the ball in front of the body with the racket.

Tracking the ball in front of you means you simply line it up with the racket. You then take a backswing as the ball bounces, a technique that is crucial to timing the ball well.

REMEMBER
Track the ball
with the racket

Upper body has turned naturally

Both hands on racket

Track with the strings

Track with the racket butt

Forehand: Track the ball with the racket in front. Hold with both hands, until the ball bounces.

Backhand: Track with the racket butt. Don't let go with the non-dominant hand until you're ready to swing.

Strike the pose

The next step involves developing the finish on each shot, which means knowing where the racket should finish up after the ball is struck. This is known as "striking the pose". For example, with the basic forehand topspin, the racket finishes up over the shoulder.

As you read on you will notice that each stroke illustrates exactly where the shot finishes after contact with the ball. Again, you can first learn these finishes just by using your hands.

Keep watching the ball, even after you've hit it

Transfer your body weight from one leg to the other as you hit the ball

REMEMBER
Always
finish

Get a grip

When you do come to learn with the racket, you will notice that top players hold the racket right at the bottom of the grip, as do the models in this book. However, you should not expect to start with this grip so soon after using just your hands. With practice and experience, grip progressions will eventually get you to this point. For example, when learning the forehand topspin, instead of holding the racket at the bottom of the grip, try holding it by the throat, and hit some shots from here first. As time goes on you can eventually slide your hand down as you start to feel more comfortable. You can do this with every shot you play.

REMEMBER
Choose the right
grip for you

Many coaches are at loggerheads with each other as to which grips are best to use for various shots. You may get your head spun as to which you should use too. However, by examining the grips available for use on different shots you can choose whichever one feels good for you. Trying out all of the grips will inform you not only of which are the best for you, but also of how you might use different grips for shots of differing height. For example, on a forehand topspin you may use an eastern grip for forehands that bounce up to below shoulder height, but then move your grip further around to a semi- or even a full western grip for shoulder height and above.

Rafael Nadal
demonstrates a
powerful two-handed
topspin backhand.

Continental/hammer grip

This grip is used for a variety of shots. Notice how the thumb and index finger straddle the grip from both sides.

On the serve this grip provides natural flexibility and pronation when hitting, and will allow you to spin the ball, whereas any other grip may hinder you.

This grip is normally employed in the volley because you can play a forehand or backhand volley without having to change your grip, which is useful, especially when the ball comes at you at 80 kilometres (50 miles) an hour. It also lets you naturally open the racket face when volleying.

It is possible to hit a topspin forehand and backhand with this grip, although the amount of topspin you will generate is marginal, and the chances of the ball flying out are increased.

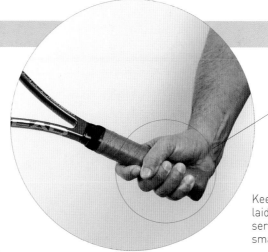

Wrist is laid off slightly with the index finger acting as a "trigger finger"

Used for

- Serve
- Smash
- Volley
- Slice
- Drop shot
- Forehand topspin

Keep wrist laid in for serves or smashes.

Wrist is laid off for all other shots.

Eastern forehand grip

This grip is similar to a shaking-hands grip, and you would normally use it for hitting a forehand topspin.

The angle of the grip allows the racket face to close more than a continental grip, so there is less chance of the ball flying out when you are brushing up the back of it.

Top players have been known to use this grip for a forehand volley as well.

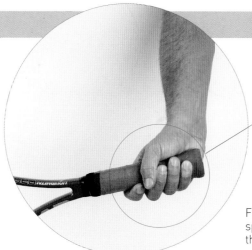

Hold as if you were shaking hands; the hand is slightly off-centre

Laid off wrist: This means the wrist is angled backwards, or "cocked".
Laid in wrist: The wrist is straighter, more in line with the arm or angled slightly forwards.

Used for

- Forehand topspin
- Forehand drive volley
- Forehand topspin lob
- Forehand volley

Fingers spread up the grip.

Wrist is laid off.

Semi-western grip

This is perhaps the most commonly used forehand topspin grip, with the hand sitting just behind the racket grip. With this grip you can usually hit an effective forehand topspin at any height and on any surface.

The grip also increases the amount of rotation on the ball, allowing more safety when you accelerate the strings up the back of the ball. It is also great for younger players starting out, because they can use it on high balls, which could arrive in abundance for small children.

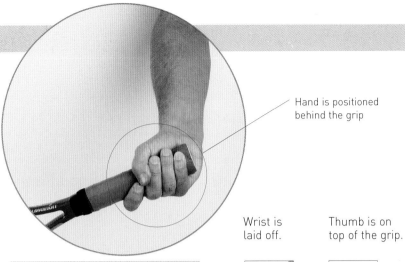

Hand is positioned behind the grip

Wrist is laid off.

Thumb is on top of the grip.

Used for

- Forehand topspin
- Forehand drive volley
- Forehand topspin lob

Full western grip

This is an extreme forehand grip with the hand almost underneath the racket grip.

It is commonly used by clay-court players, and small junior players who continually have to hit head-height balls. This grip produces large amounts of topspin.

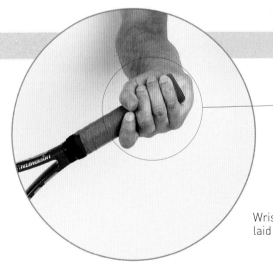

The hand is in a more extreme position, underneath the grip

Wrist is laid off.

Hand is right underneath the grip.

Used for

- Forehand smash
- Forehand topspin
- Forehand drive volley
- Forehand topspin lob

One-handed topspin backhand grip

The grip is held as if it were a bicycle handlebar, with the wrist laid off and the knuckles on top

Here you can see the nature of the one-handed topspin grip. There is also an eastern backhand grip and a semi-western backhand grip.

The hand is more or less on top of the grip in a bicycle-grip fashion. Like the forehand grips, these grips will close the racket face as you brush up the ball, and prevent the ball from flying out.

Used for

- One-handed topspin backhand
- One-handed topspin backhand drive volley
- Backhand topspin lob

The wrist is angled so the racket is square to the ball on contact.

As with the other grips, the fingers are spread. The hand is on top of the grip.

Two-handed topspin backhand grip

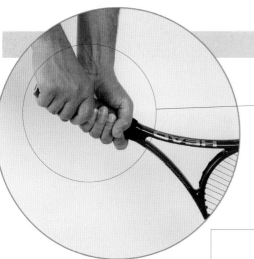

Top hand (non-dominant) is in a forehand grip; dominant hand is in the most comfortable position

This grip is used for more comfort and power on your backhand side.

The non-dominant hand is closer to the throat of the racket in a forehand grip of your choice. This hand is actually the driving force behind this shot, not your dominant hand. Your dominant hand merely sits at the bottom of the grip in any posture that's comfortable for you. Make sure that your hands are touching but not overlapping.

Used for

- Two-handed topspin backhand
- Two-handed backhand drive volley
- Backhand topspin lob

The wrist of the non-dominant hand is laid off. As with all spin-imparting grips, the racket head is below the hand.

The non-dominant hand adopts a natural grip, in this case a semi-western.

forehand topspin

FROM ABOVE

FRONT VIEW

RIGHT SIDE

BEHIND

LEFT SIDE

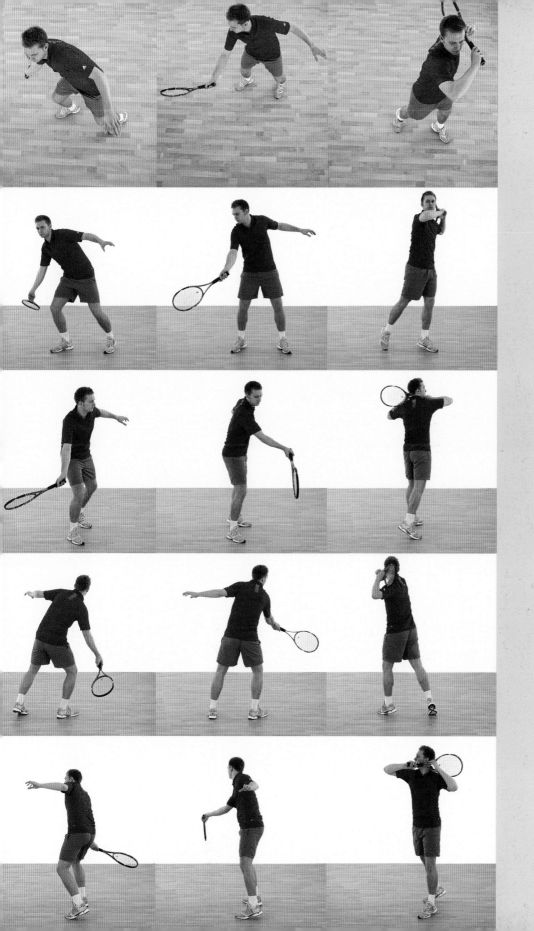

Forehand topspin

The forehand topspin is the most commonly used shot in tennis. It involves the player hitting the ball on their dominant side after the bounce, and tends to be the most favoured and most powerful shot within a player's arsenal.

Timing

All successful strokes in tennis rely on efficient timing, which involves counting from one to five fairly quickly when "waiting" for the ball. Count "one" when the ball hits the floor and "five" when you strike it.

Topspin

Topspin is essentially when the ball is struck with a brushing-up effect that causes it to rotate vigorously in a forward trajectory. This causes the ball to dip and land safely in the court.

Grips

Choose from the semi-western grip (above), the full western grip or the eastern grip (see pages 13–14).

STAGE 1

Get ready

Stand in the ready position with the racket held in front in a forehand grip. Keep knees slightly bent, ready to move fast.

THE ESSENCE OF THE SHOT

You will develop a powerful groundstroke weapon, struck with large amounts of topspin. Aim to hit the ball around 1 metre (4 feet) above the net.

Focus the eyes on the ball

Keep the head still

Relax your grip

Brush up for topspin

Always push up from the knees

Have the feet in an open stance

STAGE 2

Tracking the ball

As you wait for the ball you should also be tracking it, with the racket held in front of you.

Line up the racket with the ball

FROM THE BACK

The racket is supported with both hands while pointing slightly towards the ball.

Keep both hands on the racket

FROM THE RIGHT

The racket is tilted forwards as the ball is tracked, while being supported by the non-dominant hand.

FROM THE LEFT

The body is leaning to the forehand side as the player moves naturally towards the ball.

Transfer body weight to the outside foot

FOREHAND TOPSPIN • STAGES 1&2

Angle the racket slightly forwards

MANTRA
Track the ball

As the player tracks and moves towards the ball, notice that the non-dominant arm is positioned across the body.

FROM THE FRONT

STAGE 3
Backswing

Once the ball has bounced, take a backswing, keeping your arm and grip relaxed as you do so.

Lay the wrist off

Notice the racket supported above the hand with the wrist laid off. Also notice the dominant arm, flexed and relaxed.

FROM THE BACK

Turn the shoulders

Relax your grip

FROM THE RIGHT

The racket face is angled away from the player due to the wrist being laid off.

FROM THE LEFT

You can see the body weight pushed down onto the outside leg in an open stance.

Pull the upper body around

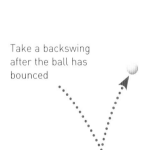

Take a backswing after the ball has bounced

As the backswing is taken, the non-dominant hand stays across the body. This hand continues to track the ball.

FROM THE FRONT

STAGE 4

Forward swing

As you start the forward swing, drop the racket head and close the racket face. The wrist remains laid off.

Racket face is closed

Have an open stance

Notice the racket head is now dropped below the hand with the wrist laid off. The racket face is closed.

FROM THE BACK

Racket head is poised to pull up to the ball

FROM THE RIGHT

The wrist is laid off with the racket butt pointing towards the ball. The racket head is below the hand.

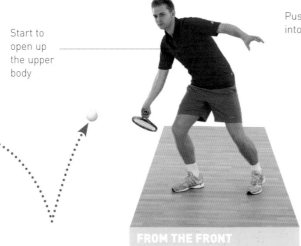

Lift the body upwards

The body weight remains on the outside leg, but now the body is lifting upwards.

FROM THE LEFT

Push your foot into the floor

Start to open up the upper body

The racket face is square and the head is slightly dropped below the hand. The body is lifting upright.

FROM THE FRONT

STAGE 5
Contact point

Contact is made with the ball via a low-to-high brushing-up effect in order to impart topspin. You can make contact at any height up to head height.

Leading with the top edge, pull the racket head upwards

Make contact with a square racket face

FROM THE BACK

Notice the racket head is square on the ball, but the head is still slightly dropped below the hand.

Keep the head still

Racket frame is perpendicular to the floor

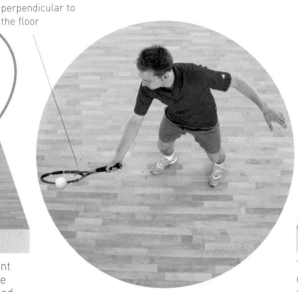

The racket will travel up over the opposite shoulder

FROM THE RIGHT

You can see the contact point comfortably in front with the elbow flexed. The racket head will now accelerate upwards.

FROM THE LEFT

The body is pushed right up on tiptoe, with body weight distributed equally on both legs.

ADDING SPIN

Use the forearm to achieve spin

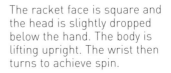

Open out the upper body

FROM THE FRONT

The racket face is square and the head is slightly dropped below the hand. The body is lifting upright. The wrist then turns to achieve spin.

STAGE 6
The finish

Finish the basic topspin with the racket over your shoulder.

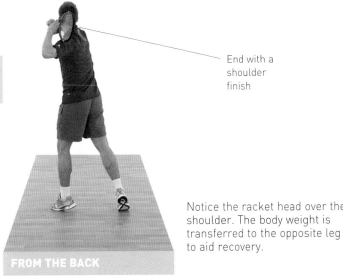

End with a shoulder finish

Notice the racket head over the shoulder. The body weight is transferred to the opposite leg to aid recovery.

FROM THE BACK

Lift your elbow up off the chest

FROM THE RIGHT

From here you can see the elbow of the dominant arm pointing directly forwards.

Fully extend the body

Notice the racket head over the opposite shoulder, and the non-dominant hand in line with the cheek.

FROM THE LEFT

Transfer body weight to the opposite foot

FOREHAND TOPSPIN • STAGES 5&6

Upper body has fully rotated

The racket butt and elbow point forwards. The player still watches the ball, anticipating the next shot.

FROM THE FRONT

MANTRA
Racket butt and elbow face opponent

TWO-HANDED TOPSPIN
backhand

FROM ABOVE

FRONT VIEW

RIGHT SIDE

BEHIND

LEFT SIDE

Two-handed topspin backhand

This is a double-fisted shot when playing a groundstroke on your non-dominant side. Many juniors use this shot, but many top professionals utilize it as well. By using two hands you will develop vast amounts of control and power.

Timing
All successful strokes in tennis rely on efficient timing, which involves counting from one to five fairly quickly when "waiting" for the ball. Count "one" when the ball hits the floor and "five" when you strike it.

Topspin
Topspin is essentially when the ball is struck with a brushing-up effect that causes it to rotate vigorously in a forward trajectory. This causes the ball to dip and land safely in the court.

Grip
A two-handed grip with hands touching and your non-dominant hand in a forehand grip.

STAGE 1
Get ready

Stand in the ready position with both hands in forehand grips and the racket in front. Keep knees slightly bent, ready to move.

THE ESSENCE OF THE SHOT

Your non-dominant hand must be the driving force behind this shot, not your dominant hand. Aim to hit the ball about 1 metre (4 feet) above the net.

Keep the head still and focus your eyes on the ball

Brush up for topspin

Rotate the trunk

Have your feet in either a closed or open stance

STAGE 2
Tracking the ball

Track the ball as it comes towards you by lining it up with the racket held in front of you.

Track the ball by lining it up with the racket

FROM THE BACK

Notice how the racket is tracking the ball in front of the player on the backhand side.

Begin to turn the shoulders

FROM THE RIGHT

From here you can see the body weight starting to shift to the backhand side.

FROM THE LEFT

Notice how the racket is tracking slightly in front of the player with both hands on the grip.

Follow the ball with the racket

Start to rotate the upper body

FROM THE FRONT

Body weight shifts to the backhand side as the player tracks the ball in front.

MANTRA
Track the ball

STAGE 3
Backswing

As the ball bounces, take a backswing with the time you have available. Make sure your supporting hand drives the racket.

Take a backswing

FROM THE BACK

The upper body has naturally turned during the backswing, and the player pushes down into the floor.

Frame is perpendicular to the ground

Turn the upper body

FROM THE RIGHT

You can either be in open or closed stance depending on the position of the ball. Let this happen naturally.

FROM THE LEFT

From here you can again see how the upper body has naturally turned during the backswing. Hands are close together on the grip.

Relax the non-dominant wrist

Push your body weight down into the floor

The player's eyes are on the ball, focusing purely on the timing and spin of the shot.

FROM THE FRONT

STAGE 4

Dropping the racket head

Before driving the racket head up to the ball, drop the head below the wrists to get lift and topspin.

Drop the racket head before brushing up the back of the ball

The body weight is loaded on the outside foot

The racket is dropped prior to acceleration up the back of the ball, to achieve lift and spin.

FROM THE BACK

Keep the wrists laid off

FROM THE RIGHT

You can clearly see the racket head dropped below the wrists and the racket face slightly tilted forwards (closed).

FROM THE LEFT

Notice how the upper body is still turned. The racket head is slightly below the hands, and the racket face is closed.

Point the front shoulder towards the ball

Prepare to vigorously unwind the upper body

Approach the ball with the racket from low to high

At this point the player is about to accelerate the racket head up the back of the ball for topspin.

FROM THE FRONT

STAGE 5
Contact point

Count "one" on the bounce followed by a brisk count, brushing up on the ball when you reach "five".

Leading with the top edge, pull the racket head upwards

Take an open stance but be ready to step in if it feels necessary

Brush up the back of the ball for topspin

FROM THE BACK

The racket head remains slightly below the hands on contact as the player pulls the racket head up.

Unwind the upper body

FROM THE RIGHT

The body is lifted as the player makes contact with the ball in front.

Start to lift the body

The player contacts the ball from a low-to-high swing and pulls the racket head up.

FROM THE LEFT

ADDING SPIN

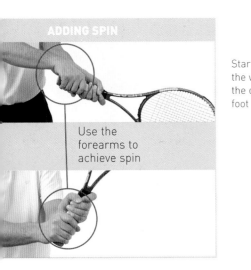

Use the forearms to achieve spin

Start to shift the weight to the opposite foot

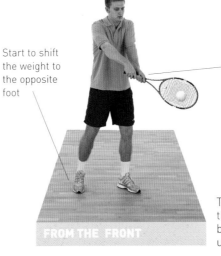

Pull the racket up with the non-dominant hand

FROM THE FRONT

The racket is fairly square at the point of contact with the ball. The strings are brushing up the ball to create spin.

STAGE 6
The finish

After brushing up the ball, the racket head is pulled up over the opposite shoulder with the non-dominant hand.

End the shot with a shoulder finish

FROM THE BACK

The racket frame is perpendicular to the floor

Notice how the player's body weight has now transferred back to the opposite leg during the finish.

FROM THE RIGHT

As the racket has finished over the shoulder, notice how the elbows are off the chest and pointing forwards.

The body weight is now on the opposite leg

FROM THE LEFT

You can clearly see the body weight now transferred to the opposite leg as the player finishes the shot.

The upper body has fully unwound

The player has finished the shot over the shoulder, but still watches the ball, anticipating the next shot.

FROM THE FRONT

TWO-HANDED TOPSPIN BACKHAND • STAGES 5&6

MANTRA
Finish with racket butt and elbow facing opponent

ONE-HANDED TOPSPIN
backhand

FROM ABOVE

FRONT VIEW

RIGHT SIDE

BEHIND

LEFT SIDE

One-handed topspin backhand

This is a single-handed shot when playing a groundstroke on your non-dominant side. Using one hand on your backhand significantly increases your reach capacity.

Timing

All successful strokes in tennis rely on efficient timing, which involves counting from one to five fairly quickly when "waiting" for the ball. Count "one" when the ball hits the floor and "five" when you strike it.

Topspin

Topspin is essentially when the ball is struck with a brushing-up effect that causes it to rotate vigorously in a forward trajectory. This causes the ball to dip and land safely in the court.

Grips

Choose from the eastern grip, the semi-western grip and the continental grip (see pages 13 and 14). Imagine you are holding a "bicycle" grip with your knuckles on top.

STAGE 1
Get ready

Stand in the ready position with the racket in front and with the non-dominant hand supporting the racket throat. Keep knees slightly bent, ready to move.

THE ESSENCE OF THE SHOT

Just like other topspin shots, brush up the back of the ball and lift it 1 metre (4 feet) above the net.

Gain power by squeezing the shoulder blades

Brush up for topspin

THE STROKES

Tracking the ball

Find your grip and track the ball by pointing the racket butt towards it.

Track the ball with the racket butt

Notice how the racket butt is pointing towards the ball in front of the player on the backhand side.

FROM THE BACK

Position the racket head above the wrist

Start to rotate the upper body

FROM THE RIGHT

From here you can see the body weight starting to shift to the backhand side.

FROM THE LEFT

Notice how the non-dominant hand supports the racket throat, and how the wrist is cocked.

Watch the ball

Push down through the foot

Point the racket butt at the ball

MANTRA
Point the racket butt

FROM THE FRONT

The body weight shifts to the backhand side as the player tracks the ball in front.

STAGE 3
Backswing

As the ball bounces, take a backswing with the time you have available. As with all shots, push down into the floor.

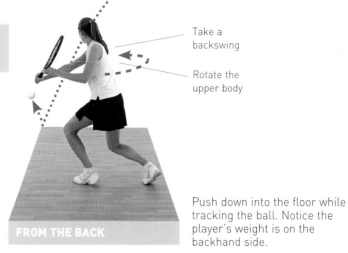

Take a backswing

Rotate the upper body

FROM THE BACK

Push down into the floor while tracking the ball. Notice the player's weight is on the backhand side.

The back is fully visible from the side

FROM THE RIGHT

You can be in open or closed stance, depending on the position of the ball. Let this happen naturally.

Put your body weight onto the outside leg

FROM THE LEFT

Notice how the upper body has naturally turned during the backswing, and how the wrist is cocked.

Point the front shoulder towards the ball

The non-dominant hand is still supporting the throat of the racket

FROM THE FRONT

The player's eyes are on the ball, focusing purely on the timing and spin of the shot.

ONE-HANDED TOPSPIN BACKHAND • STAGES 2&3

STAGE 4
Contact point

Count "one" on the bounce followed by a brisk count, brushing up on the ball when you reach "five".

Fully extend the body as you brush up

Brush up the back of the ball for topspin

The non-dominant hand is released and the racket head remains slightly below the hand as it brushes up on contact.

FROM THE BACK

Unwind the upper body

Keep the head still

FROM THE RIGHT

Lift the body as you make contact with the ball in front.

Contact the ball from a low-to-high swing, pulling the racket head up.

FROM THE LEFT

ADDING SPIN

Use the forearm to achieve spin

Keep watching the ball

Push up through the legs

Leading with the top edge, pull the racket head upwards

FROM THE FRONT

The racket is fairly square at the point of contact with the ball.

STAGE 5
The finish

After brushing up the ball, the racket head finishes high. The shoulder blades are squeezed together for power output.

Utilize the "Statue of Liberty" finish

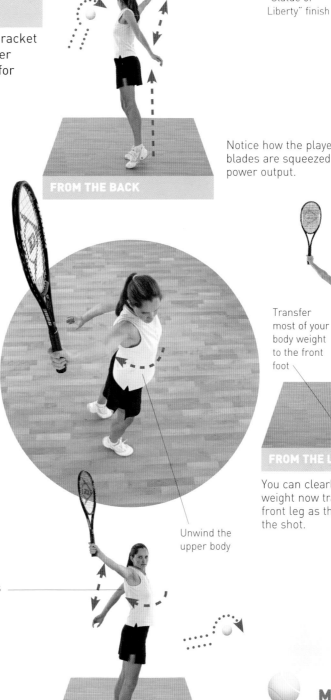

Notice how the player's shoulder blades are squeezed together for power output.

Pull the non-dominant hand back behind the body

FROM THE BACK

Step into the ball and finish in a high "Statue of Liberty" pose.

FROM THE RIGHT

Transfer most of your body weight to the front foot

FROM THE LEFT

You can clearly see the body weight now transferred to the front leg as the player finishes the shot.

Unwind the upper body

Squeeze the shoulder blades together

The player has finished the shot but still watches the ball, anticipating the next shot.

FROM THE FRONT

MANTRA
Finish high in a "Statue of Liberty" pose

ONE-HANDED TOPSPIN BACKHAND • STAGES 4&5

ONE-HANDED slice backhand

FROM ABOVE

FRONT VIEW

RIGHT SIDE

BEHIND

LEFT SIDE

One-handed slice backhand

This is a single-handed shot when playing a groundstroke on your non-dominant side. Using one hand on your backhand significantly increases your reach capacity. Slice is used primarily as a defensive shot when the player is under pressure, but it can also be used aggressively, as with an approach shot or drop shot.

Timing

All successful strokes in tennis rely on efficient timing, which involves counting from one to five fairly quickly when "waiting" for the ball. Count "one" when the ball hits the floor and "five" when you strike it.

Slice

Slice is when the ball is struck with a combination of side- and backspin.

Grip
The continental grip is normally used for this shot (see page 13).

STAGE 1
Get ready

THE ESSENCE OF THE SHOT

The essence of this shot is to keep the ball low over the net and low on the bounce.

Stand in the ready position, racket in front with the non-dominant hand supporting the racket throat. Keep knees slightly bent, ready to move.

Keep the head still and focus on the ball

Hit slice, a combination of side- and backspin

Fully extend the leading arm

Step towards the ball if it feels more comfortable

STAGE 2
Tracking the ball

Track the ball by lining it up with the racket butt pointing towards it.

Track the ball with the racket butt

Lean into the outside foot as you play the ball

Notice how the racket butt is pointing towards the ball in front of the player on the backhand side.

FROM THE BACK

FROM THE RIGHT

From here you can see the body weight starting to shift to the backhand side.

Open racket face

FROM THE LEFT

Notice how the non-dominant hand supports the racket throat and the wrist is cocked.

Start to rotate the upper body as you track the ball

The player's body weight shifts to the backhand side while tracking the ball in front.

FROM THE FRONT

ONE-HANDED SLICE BACKHAND • STAGES 1&2

MANTRA
Point the racket butt

STAGE 3
Backswing

As the ball bounces, take a backswing with the time you have available. As with all shots, push down into the floor.

Take a backswing

Transfer the weight

FROM THE BACK

The player is pushing down into the floor while tracking the ball. The weight is on the backhand side.

Racket face is pulled back

FROM THE RIGHT

You can be in an open or closed stance, depending on the position of the ball. Let this happen naturally.

Shoulders are aligned

Notice how the racket head is laid back, supported by the non-dominant hand, and how the racket face is open.

FROM THE LEFT

Fully rotate the upper body

The wrist is laid off

The player's eyes are on the ball, focusing purely on the timing and spin of the shot.

FROM THE FRONT

STAGE 4
Contact point

Count "one" on the bounce, hit down and across the underside of the ball when you reach "five".

Upper body starts to unwind

Hit down and across the ball for back- and sidespin

FROM THE BACK

Keep the non-dominant hand behind you

The player has now released the non-dominant hand. The racket face is slightly open on contact.

Racket face is open

FROM THE RIGHT

Step into the ball as you make contact in front.

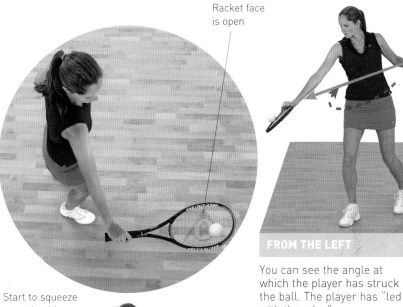

FROM THE LEFT

You can see the angle at which the player has struck the ball. The player has "led with the edge".

ADDING SLICE

Pull the racket butt in to achieve slice

Start to squeeze your shoulders together

The racket face is slightly open on contact as the player slices the strings under the ball.

Pull the racket butt in

FROM THE FRONT

MANTRA
Hit down and across

STAGE 5
The finish

As you finish the shot, your shoulder blades should be completely squeezed together.

Squeeze the shoulder blades together on finish

FROM THE BACK

The shoulder blades squeeze together at the finish.

Body weight is on the front foot

Pull back the hands

FROM THE RIGHT

The player pulls up from her supporting leg after the shot.

Shoulders are aligned

FROM THE LEFT

You can clearly see the player's shoulders rolled back.

The racket arm has pulled across the ball

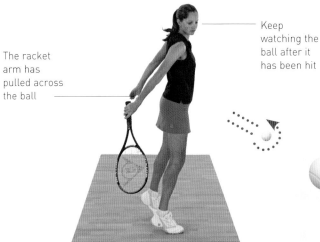

Keep watching the ball after it has been hit

FROM THE FRONT

Once finished, watch the ball as you recover to the ready position.

MANTRA
Squeeze those shoulder blades

ONE-HANDED BACKHAND drop shot

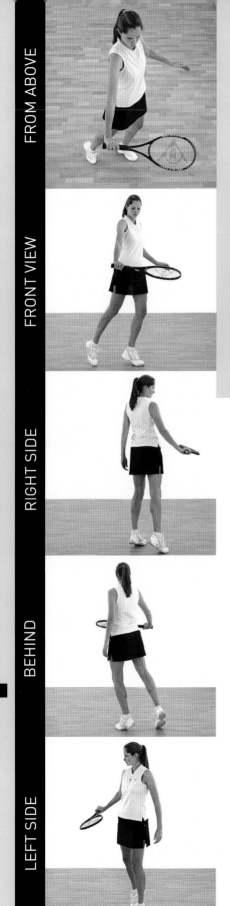

FROM ABOVE

FRONT VIEW

RIGHT SIDE

BEHIND

LEFT SIDE

One-handed backhand drop shot

To catch out players who often play from the back of the court, you can play a drop shot, essentially a slice backhand with an open racket face that causes the ball to drop just on the opposite side of the net.

Contact point

Notice how open the racket face is. You must get right under the ball and accelerate through this shot, not slow up on it.

Grip the racket like a handlebar

Focus on the ball

SIDESPIN
slice serve

FROM ABOVE

FRONT VIEW

RIGHT SIDE

BEHIND

LEFT SIDE

Sidespin slice serve

This type of serve imparts sidespin on the side of the ball, thus making the ball swerve in flight. It is a useful tool for either a first or second serve. You can also hit across the back of the ball and hit what we call a "heavy" serve, which is thought by many to be the flat serve.

Timing

All successful strokes in tennis rely on efficient timing, when you "wait" for the ball and count from one to five fairly quickly. Count "one" when the ball leaves your hand, then strike the ball on "five".

Slice

Slice is when the ball is struck with sidespin.

Grip
The continental grip is normally used for this shot (see page 13).

STAGE 1
Address the serve

Stand at roughly 45 degrees to the baseline with the ball and racket in front of you. At this point you should be taking careful aim at where you want your serve to land. The wrist is laid in.

THE ESSENCE OF THE SHOT

To hit the serve up and over the net, into the service box, with sidespin.

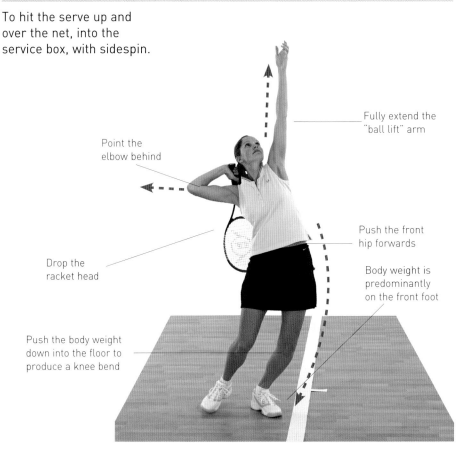

Point the elbow behind

Drop the racket head

Push the body weight down into the floor to produce a knee bend

Fully extend the "ball lift" arm

Push the front hip forwards

Body weight is predominantly on the front foot

Bring both arms
up together

STAGE 2
Bringing both hands up together

To start the serve, bring both hands
up together, with racket arm bent
at the elbow and ball arm extended.

FROM THE BACK

Hold the ball in the
fingertips

FROM THE RIGHT

Notice the knees start to bend
as the front foot pushes down.

Extend the ball arm and bend
the racket arm. Push down
into the floor.

Keep the wrist
turned in

FROM THE LEFT

Notice the straight line created
by the ball arm and the upper
arm of the racket arm.

Turn the
upper body
slightly to
the right
when lifting
the ball

Starting point
of the ball arm

Notice the ball arm has been
raised from across the body, not
straight out in front of the player.

FROM THE FRONT

MANTRA
Bring both hands
up together

Ball rises and falls in an arc towards your forehead

STAGE 3
Point the racket butt

Drop the racket head and point the racket butt at the ball to produce power on the serve.

Point the racket butt

FROM THE BACK

The ball has now been released and the racket butt is pointing up at it. The knees are well bent.

Watch the ball all the time

Push down into the floor

FROM THE RIGHT

From here the player is ready to explode up into the serve. Note the weight on the front foot.

FROM THE LEFT

Even though the ball is now in the air, the player still maintains a straight ball arm, tracking the ball.

The server's body is side on — some top players would be even further around to the right

Point the racket butt at the ball

The racket frame faces the net

With eyes on the ball, the player is poised to explode up into the serve.

FROM THE FRONT

STAGE 4

Contact point – exploding upwards

Now you explode up into the serve, throwing the racket frame across the ball to impart sidespin.

Bring the racket strings across the ball to cause the curve and spin

The player has now fully extended, and advanced players should be lifting off the floor.

FROM THE BACK

Unwind the hips and shoulders

Cover the ball

Push up from your front foot

FROM THE RIGHT

The player is throwing the racket frame from left to right across the ball. The left hand is across the middle of the body.

FROM THE LEFT

Note the angle of the player's wrist, slightly tilted forwards in order to "cover" the ball.

Eyes on the ball

Fully extend the body

Watch the ball as you hit up and across it. Serves are hit up, not down.

FROM THE FRONT

SIDESPIN SLICE SERVE • STAGES 3&4

MANTRA
Reach up

STAGE 5
Throwing the racket frame

As you hit up and across the ball, the wrist will turn out to the side.

Throw the racket frame out to the side

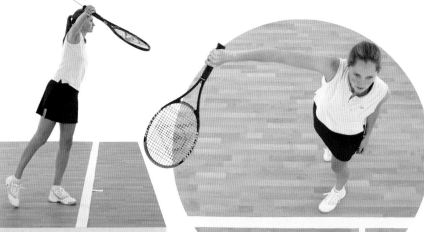

FROM THE BACK

Here you can clearly see the twist of the wrist.

Snap the wrist out to the side

FROM THE RIGHT

When hitting sidespin the racket head frame is thrown out to the right side.

FROM THE LEFT

The player has landed on the front foot. Advanced players may even land inside the court after their serve.

MANTRA
Hit up and across the ball

Let the body unwind

FROM THE FRONT

The player continues to watch the ball in order to track the opponent's return.

STAGE 6
The finish

After the sidespin serve, the racket tends to finish around the opposite side, at about waist height.

Finish the serve

FROM THE BACK

The racket can also finish in front of the player

Note the racket head finishing around the player's opposite side, at about waist height.

Shoulders finish square to the net

FROM THE RIGHT

The player has elected to step forwards, maybe to attack a short return from the opponent.

FROM THE LEFT

You can clearly see the player's racket finish as she advances down the court.

The upper body has unwound fully

After the serve, the player is always alert and ready to deal with the next shot.

FROM THE FRONT

SIDESPIN SLICE SERVE • STAGES 5&6

TOPSLICE/
topspin serve

FROM ABOVE

FRONT VIEW

RIGHT SIDE

BEHIND

LEFT SIDE

Topslice/topspin serve

This type of serve imparts top- and sidespin on the ball, thus giving the ball greater clearance over the net. It is a useful tool, especially for a second serve. The topspin serve is technically similar to the sidespin serve but the bounce of the ball is different, thus producing a different outcome.

Timing

All successful strokes in tennis rely on efficient timing, when you "wait" for the ball and count from one to five fairly quickly. Count "one" when the ball leaves your hand, then strike the ball on "five".

Topslice

This happens when the ball is struck with a combination of top- and sidespin.

Grip

The continental grip is normally used for this shot (see page 13).

(see page 13)

STAGE 1

Address the serve

Stand at roughly 45 degrees to the baseline with the ball and racket in front of you. At this point you should be taking careful aim at where you want your serve to land. The wrist is laid in.

THE ESSENCE OF THE SHOT

You want to hit the serve up and over the net into the service box with top- and sidespin.

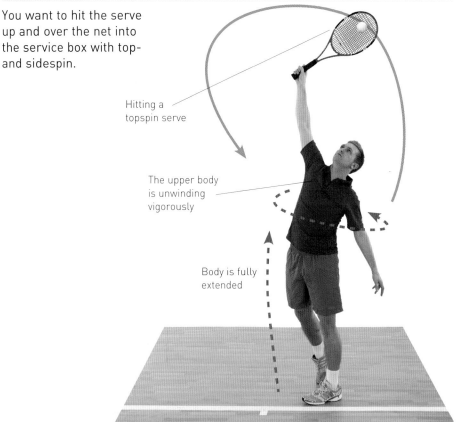

Hitting a topspin serve

The upper body is unwinding vigorously

Body is fully extended

STAGE 2

Bringing both hands up together

To start the serve, bring both hands up together, with racket arm bent at the elbow and ball arm extended.

Bring both arms up together

Keep your wrist turned in

FROM THE BACK

Form a straight line from shoulder to shoulder

FROM THE RIGHT

Notice the knees start to bend as the front foot pushes down.

Extend the ball arm and bend the racket arm. Push down into the floor.

Hold the ball in your fingertips

Begin to arch the back

FROM THE LEFT

Notice the straight line created from the ball arm and the upper arm of the racket arm.

Turn your body slightly to the right

Starting point of the ball arm

The ball arm is raised from across the body, not straight out in front of the player.

FROM THE FRONT

MANTRA
Bring both hands up together

STAGE 3
Point the racket butt

By dropping the racket head and pointing the racket butt at the ball, you will produce power on the serve. The ball needs to be placed towards the back of the head.

The ball is released slightly late so it falls in an arc towards the back of the head

Point the racket butt

The ball has been released and the racket butt is pointing up at it. Notice that the knees are well bent.

FROM THE BACK

The now-dominant elbow points behind

Push down into the floor

Keep your ball arm extended

Always watch the ball

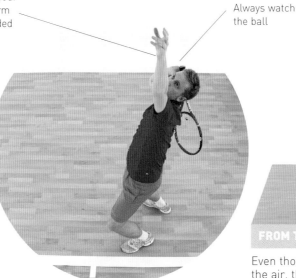

From here, with weight on the front foot, the player is ready to explode up into the serve.

FROM THE RIGHT

Even though the ball is now in the air, the player still maintains a straight ball arm, and tracks the ball.

FROM THE LEFT

Point the racket butt

Drop the racket head before throwing it up towards the ball

Turn sideways with the left shoulder pointing towards the net

With eyes on the ball, the player is poised to explode up into the serve.

FROM THE FRONT

STAGE 4
Contact point – exploding upwards

Explode up into the serve and throw the racket frame up the back of the ball to impart top- and sidespin.

Extend upwards

The player has now fully extended, and advanced players should be lifting off the floor.

FROM THE BACK

Watch the ball

Rise up, out of your front foot

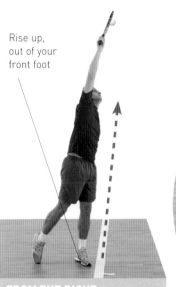

FROM THE RIGHT

The player throws the racket frame from low to high, up and across the ball.

Note the angle of the player's wrist. It is slightly tilted forwards in order to "cover" the ball.

FROM THE LEFT

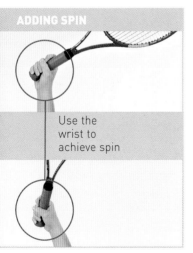

ADDING SPIN

Use the wrist to achieve spin

Unwind the upper body

Watch the ball as you hit up and across it. Serves are hit up, not hit down.

FROM THE FRONT

MANTRA
Push up off the floor

STAGE 5
Throwing the racket frame

As you hit up and across the ball, the wrist will turn out to the side.

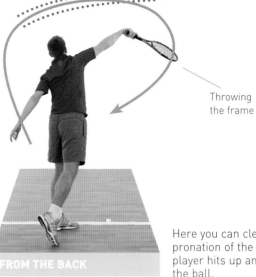

Throwing the frame

Here you can clearly see the pronation of the wrist as the player hits up and across the ball.

FROM THE BACK

The back foot is used as a support

Snap the wrist

FROM THE RIGHT

When hitting top- and sidespin the racket head frame is thrown out to the right side.

The player landed on the front foot. Advanced players may even land inside the court after their serve.

FROM THE LEFT

The upper body has fully unwound

 MANTRA
Brush up and across the ball

Finish on the front foot

FROM THE FRONT

The player continues to watch the ball in order to track the opponent's return.

STAGE 6
The finish

After the topspin serve, the racket tends to finish around the opposite side, at about waist height.

Finishing the serve

FROM THE BACK

The racket can finish at the front or at the side as shown here

Note the racket head finishing around the player's opposite side, at about waist height.

FROM THE RIGHT

The player has elected to step forwards, maybe to attack a short return from the opponent.

FROM THE LEFT

You can clearly see the player's racket finish as he advances down the court.

After the serve, the player is always alert and ready to deal with the next shot.

FROM THE FRONT

slice forehand

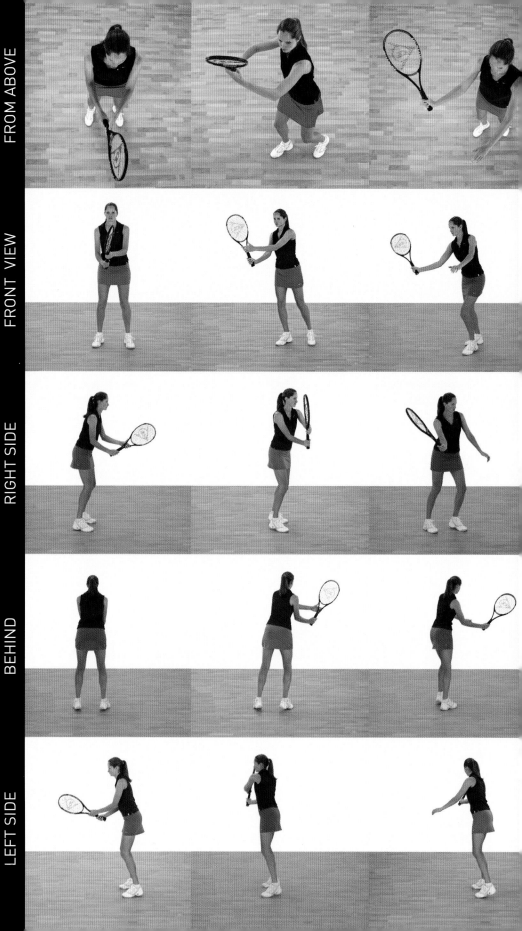

Slice forehand

This is a single-handed shot when playing a groundstroke on your dominant side. Slice is used primarily as a defensive shot when the player is under pressure, but it can also be used aggressively, such as in an approach shot or drop shot.

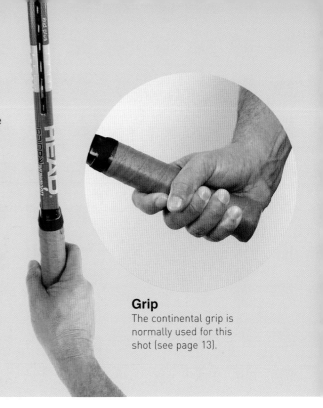

Timing

All successful strokes in tennis rely on efficient timing. When "waiting" for the ball count from one to five fairly quickly. Count "one" when the ball hits the floor and "five" when you strike it.

Slice

Slice is when the ball is struck with a combination of side- and backspin.

Grip

The continental grip is normally used for this shot (see page 13).

STAGE 1
Get ready

Stand in the ready position, racket in front with the non-dominant hand supporting the racket throat. Keep knees slightly bent, ready to move.

THE ESSENCE OF THE SHOT

The essence of this shot is to keep the ball low over the net and low on the bounce.

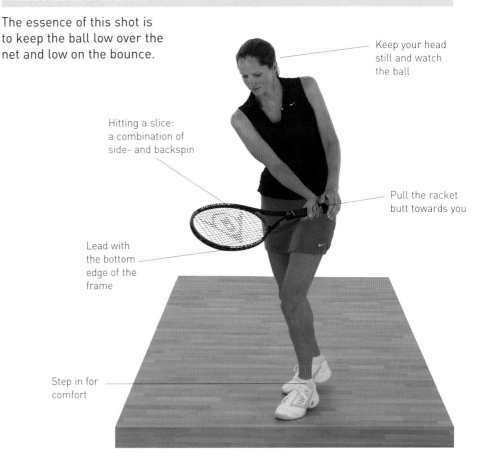

Keep your head still and watch the ball

Hitting a slice: a combination of side- and backspin

Pull the racket butt towards you

Lead with the bottom edge of the frame

Step in for comfort

STAGE 2
Tracking the ball

Track the ball as it comes towards you by lining it up with the racket.

Track the ball

FROM THE BACK

Notice the racket tracking the ball in front of the player on the forehand side.

Track the ball with both hands on the racket

FROM THE RIGHT

From here you can see the body weight starting to shift to the forehand side.

FROM THE LEFT

Notice how the non-dominant hand supports the racket throat, and the wrist is cocked.

The upper body is starting to rotate

The player's body weight shifts to the forehand side as she tracks the ball in front.

FROM THE FRONT

MANTRA
Track it with the racket

STAGE 3
Backswing

As the ball bounces, take a backswing with the time you have available. Like all shots, push down into the floor.

Starting the backswing

The player's non-dominant hand starts to push the racket back.

Open racket face

Keep your head still

FROM THE RIGHT

You can either be in an open or closed stance, depending on the position of the ball. Let this happen naturally.

FROM THE LEFT

The racket head is laid back and the racket face starts to open.

Fully turn the upper body

Step in for comfort

FROM THE FRONT

The player's eyes are on the ball, focusing purely on the timing and spin of the shot.

STAGE 4

Contact point

After counting "one" on the bounce, hit down and across the underside of the ball when you reach "five".

Hit down and across the ball for back- and sidespin

FROM THE BACK

The player has led with the edge of the racket. The racket face is slightly open on contact.

The upper body unwinds naturally

FROM THE RIGHT

The player steps into the ball and makes contact in front.

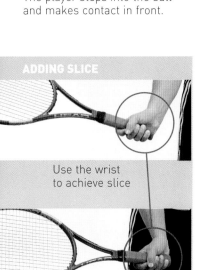

FROM THE LEFT

You can see the angle at which the player has struck the ball, leading with the edge of the racket.

ADDING SLICE

Use the wrist to achieve slice

Keep your forearm slightly flexed

The wrist is laid off

The player is watching the ball intently as the strings slide under it.

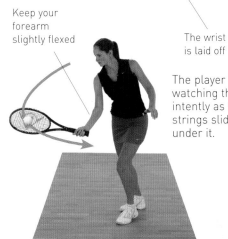

FROM THE FRONT

MANTRA
Hit down and across

SLICE FOREHAND • STAGES 3&4

STAGE 5
The finish

Pull the racket across the line of the ball to impart side- and backspin.

Pull the racket butt in

FROM THE BACK

Pull the racket butt in towards you to get power and spin.

Keep your head still

FROM THE RIGHT

Use your shoulder muscles to pull the racket in towards you.

FROM THE LEFT

You can clearly see the racket butt being pulled in towards the player.

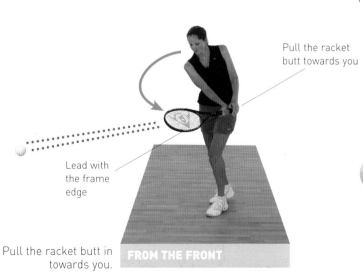

Pull the racket butt towards you

Lead with the frame edge

Pull the racket butt in towards you.

FROM THE FRONT

MANTRA
Pull that racket butt in

Forehand drop shot

To catch out players who often play from the back of the court, you can play a drop shot, essentially a slice forehand with an open racket face that causes the ball to drop just on the opposite side of the net.

Contact point

Notice how open the racket face is. You must get right under the ball and accelerate through this shot, not slow up on it.

The upper body unwinds

Keep your head still

Pull the racket butt towards you

Step forwards for comfort

HIGH forehand volley

FROM ABOVE

FRONT VIEW

RIGHT SIDE

BEHIND

LEFT SIDE

High forehand volley

This shot is normally used around the net area when there is little chance of the ball bouncing before the player hits it. The player is really looking to win the point with a volley, especially a volley at head height.

Timing
All successful strokes in tennis rely on efficient timing, when you "wait" for the ball and count from one to five fairly quickly. Count "one" on the opponent's strike and volley the ball when you reach "five".

Spin
Since volley techniques are similar to slice shots, the spin used is normally back- or sidespin, or both.

Grips
The continental grip is normally used for this shot, though some players use the eastern forehand grip (see page 13).

(see page 13)

STAGE 1
Get ready

Stand in the ready position with the racket held in front in a continental grip. Keep knees slightly bent, ready to move fast.

THE ESSENCE OF THE SHOT

When you find yourself at the net, due to choice or circumstance, you must be able to win points using sound volleying technique.

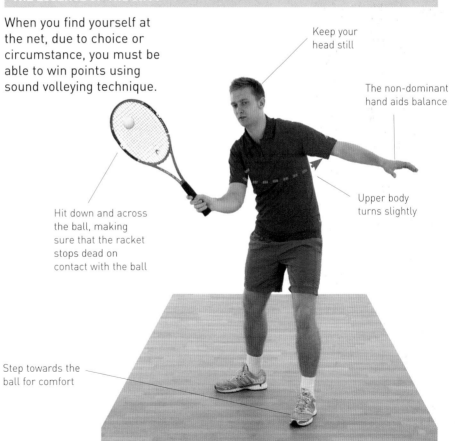

Keep your head still

The non-dominant hand aids balance

Upper body turns slightly

Hit down and across the ball, making sure that the racket stops dead on contact with the ball

Step towards the ball for comfort

STAGE 2
Tracking the ball

Track the ball with the racket held in front of you and above your hand.

Track the ball with the racket in front

Lay the racket back slightly

The racket is held above the hand and slightly laid back.

The wrist is laid off

FROM THE RIGHT

The player's body weight leans slightly to the forehand side as the ball is tracked.

FROM THE LEFT

The player moves naturally towards the ball, causing the body to lean to the forehand side.

The upper body turns slightly

MANTRA
Track the ball

FROM THE FRONT

As the player tracks and moves towards the ball, notice that the non-dominant hand aids balance.

STAGE 3
Contact point

Meet the ball as you reach "five" on your timing count. Make sure that you stop on the ball.

Stop the racket on the ball

The hips unwind

FROM THE BACK

You can see that the wrist is laid off as the player pulls the racket butt in slightly towards him.

Keep your head still

FROM THE RIGHT

The player stops the racket on the ball. The racket face is slightly open.

FROM THE LEFT

The player has adopted a partially closed stance. Let your feet move naturally to the ball.

HIGH FOREHAND VOLLEY • STAGES 2&3

The upper body turns slightly

Step forwards for comfort

The player is intently watching the ball as contact is made.

FROM THE FRONT

MANTRA
Stop on the ball and return to ready position

FOREHAND
drop volley

Forehand drop volley

One way to really catch out your opponent is to stun the ball over the net via a drop volley. Just by opening the racket face more than usual, you can undercut the ball so it just drops on the other side of the net.

Contact point

You can see just how open the racket face is in order to get under the ball.

Get under the ball

FROM THE FRONT

The finish

Finish the drop volley by slightly pulling the racket butt in towards you.

Keep your head still

Pull the racket butt towards you

FROM THE FRONT

MANTRA
Pull that racket butt in

LOW
forehand volley

FROM ABOVE

FRONT VIEW

RIGHT SIDE

BEHIND

LEFT SIDE

Low forehand volley

This shot is normally used around the net area when there is little chance of the ball bouncing before the player hits it. The ball is met by the player below net height, forcing the player to volley upwards.

Timing
All successful strokes in tennis rely on efficient timing, when you "wait" for the ball and count from one to five fairly quickly. Count "one" on the opponent's strike and volley the ball when you reach "five".

Spin
Since volley techniques are similar to slice shots, the spin used is normally back- or sidespin, or both.

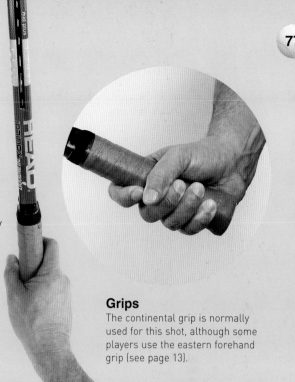

Grips
The continental grip is normally used for this shot, although some players use the eastern forehand grip (see page 13).

STAGE 1
Get ready

Stand in the ready position with the racket held in front in a continental grip. Keep knees slightly bent, ready to move fast.

THE ESSENCE OF THE SHOT

When you find yourself at the net, due to choice or circumstance, you must be able to win points using sound volleying technique.

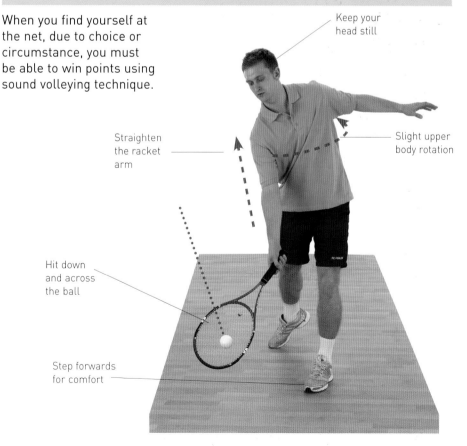

Keep your head still

Straighten the racket arm

Slight upper body rotation

Hit down and across the ball

Step forwards for comfort

STAGE 2
Tracking the ball

Track the ball with the racket held in front of you and above your hand.

Track the ball

FROM THE BACK

The racket is held above the hand and slightly laid back, with the racket face open.

Keep your head still

Get down to the ball

FROM THE RIGHT

When tracking the ball the player's knees are bent and lean towards the forehand side.

FROM THE LEFT

As the player moves naturally towards the ball, the body leans to the forehand side.

Open racket face

Watch the ball

MANTRA
Track the ball

FROM THE FRONT

As the player tracks and moves towards the ball, notice that the non-dominant hand aids balance.

STAGE 3
Contact point

Meet the ball as you reach "five" on your timing count. Make sure that you stop on the ball.

Stop the racket on the ball

FROM THE BACK

As the player hits down with the open racket face, notice the body lifting naturally.

Allow your body to lift naturally

FROM THE RIGHT

The player stops the racket on the ball. The racket face is more open than with a high volley (see pages 70–73).

Watch the ball

Contact in front

FROM THE LEFT

The player has adopted a closed stance. Let your feet move naturally to the ball.

Slight upper body rotation

The player intently watches the ball as contact is made.

FROM THE FRONT

MANTRA
Stop on the ball and return to ready position

LOW FOREHAND VOLLEY • STAGES 2&3

STAGE ONE

STAGE TWO

STAGE THREE

STAGE FOUR

Forehand half volley

There will be times, when you are close to the net, when the ball will hit the floor before you hit it. This may be due to the ball coming right at your feet. Because you have so little time to react, you will have to lift the ball as soon as it has hit the floor, using the half volley.

THE ESSENCE OF THE SHOT

React quickly to lift the ball as soon as it has hit the court.

Lift the ball as soon as it hits the floor

STAGE 3
Contact point

The player gets down to the ball with the racket face slightly closed in order to cover it as they lift it.

Get down to the ball

FROM THE BACK

The player's body weight is on the front foot due to the posture of her back foot.

Lean forwards from the upper body

FROM THE RIGHT

Note the angle of the racket face. It is slightly closed in order to cover the ball as it is lifted upwards.

Step forwards for comfort

FROM THE LEFT

The player's front leg is bent as she gets down to the ball to lift it.

STAGE 4
The finish

Allow your body to lift naturally with the shot.

The racket frame is perpendicular to the floor

FROM THE FRONT

The player's head remains still as she intently watches the ball and plays the shot.

FOREHAND HALF VOLLEY

82

MEDIUM
backhand volley

FROM ABOVE

FRONT VIEW

RIGHT SIDE

BEHIND

LEFT SIDE

Medium backhand volley

This shot is normally used around the net area when there is little chance of the ball bouncing before the player hits it.

Timing
All successful strokes in tennis rely on efficient timing, when you "wait" for the ball and count from one to five fairly quickly. Count "one" on the opponent's strike and volley the ball when you reach "five".

Spin
Since volley techniques are similar to slice shots, the spin used is normally back- or sidespin, or both.

Grip
The continental grip is normally used for this shot (see page 13).

(see page 13)

STAGE 1
Get ready

Stand in the ready position with the racket held in front in a continental grip. Keep knees slightly bent, ready to move fast.

THE ESSENCE OF THE SHOT

When you find yourself at the net, due to choice or circumstance, you must be able to win points using sound volleying technique.

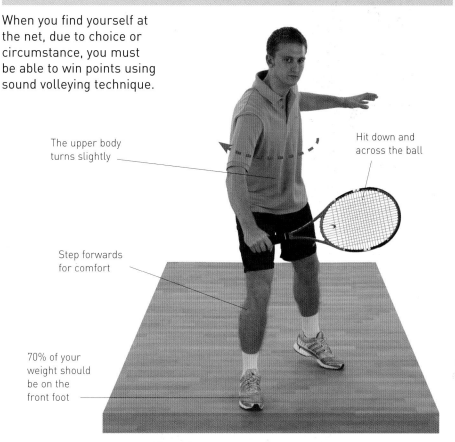

The upper body turns slightly

Hit down and across the ball

Step forwards for comfort

70% of your weight should be on the front foot

THE STROKES

Tracking the ball

Track the ball with your non-dominant hand supporting the throat of the racket, held in front of you.

Track the ball with the non-dominant hand in support

This foot is poised to step forwards

FROM THE BACK

The racket is held above the hand and slightly laid back.

Partial upper body rotation

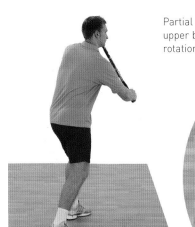

FROM THE RIGHT

The player's body weight is leaning slightly to the backhand side as he tracks the ball.

You can see the non-dominant hand supporting the throat of the racket.

FROM THE LEFT

Watch the ball

Wrist is laid off

As the player tracks and moves towards the ball, notice the racket head being held above the hand.

FROM THE FRONT

STAGE 3
Contact point

Meet the ball as you reach "five" on your timing count. Make sure that you stop on the ball.

Keep your head still

Stop the racket on the ball

FROM THE BACK

The racket face is slightly open on contact.

The non-dominant hand releases the racket

FROM THE RIGHT

The player stops the racket on the ball. The racket face is slightly open.

FROM THE LEFT

The player has adopted a partially closed stance, letting his feet move naturally to the ball.

Contact is out in front

The upper body unwinds slightly

FROM THE FRONT

The player is intently watching the ball as contact is made.

MANTRA
Stop on the ball

MEDIUM BACKHAND VOLLEY • STAGES 2&3

BACKHAND drop volley

Backhand drop volley

One way to really catch out your opponent is to stun the ball over the net via a drop volley. By opening the racket face more than usual, you can undercut the ball so it just drops on the other side of the net.

THE ESSENCE OF THE SHOT

By tilting the racket face you can drop the ball over to the other side of the net.

Watch the ball

Open racket face

Keep your elbow flexed

Cushion the ball to reduce the pace

Knees are slightly flexed

Contact point

You can see just how open the racket face is in order to get under the ball.

Get under the ball

Flex the knees slightly

FROM THE BACK

The player's body weight has shifted to the side from which she is hitting the ball.

The non-dominant arm aids balance

FROM THE RIGHT

The contact point is out in front of the player.

Open racket face

FROM THE LEFT

The racket face is open to undercut the ball for massive amounts of backspin.

Slight upper body rotation

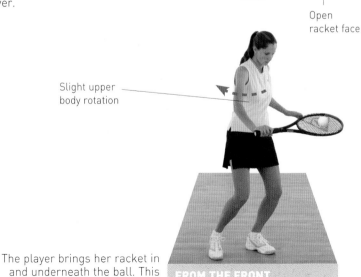

FROM THE FRONT

The player brings her racket in and underneath the ball. This action creates sidespin.

The finish

Finish the drop volley by slightly pulling the racket butt in towards you.

LOW
backhand volley

FROM ABOVE

FRONT VIEW

RIGHT SIDE

BEHIND

LEFT SIDE

Low backhand volley

This shot is normally used around the net area when there is little chance of the ball bouncing before the player hits it. The ball is met by the player below net height, forcing the player to volley upwards.

Timing
All successful strokes in tennis rely on efficient timing, when you "wait" for the ball and count from one to five fairly quickly. Count "one" on the opponent's strike and volley the ball when you reach "five".

Spin
Since volley techniques are similar to slice shots, the spin used is normally back- or sidespin, or both.

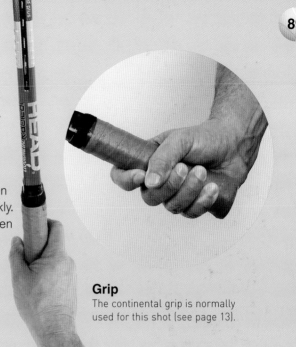

Grip
The continental grip is normally used for this shot (see page 13).

STAGE 1
Get ready

Stand in the ready position with the racket held in front in a continental grip. Keep knees slightly bent, ready to move fast.

THE ESSENCE OF THE SHOT

When you find yourself at the net, due to choice or circumstance, you must be able to win points using sound volleying technique.

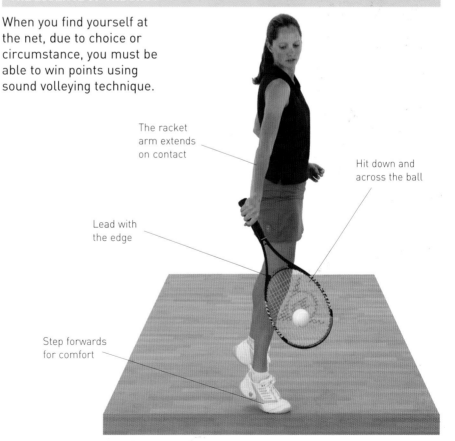

The racket arm extends on contact

Hit down and across the ball

Lead with the edge

Step forwards for comfort

STAGE 2
Tracking the ball

Track the ball with the racket held above your hand and in front of you.

Track the low ball with the racket in front

FROM THE BACK

The racket is held above the hand and slightly laid back, with the racket face open.

Keep your head still

FROM THE RIGHT

The player's knees are bent and lean towards the backhand side as she tracks the ball.

FROM THE LEFT

Notice how the non-dominant hand supports the racket as the player tracks the ball.

The upper body rotates slightly

The wrist is laid off

Step towards the ball

MANTRA
Track the ball

FROM THE FRONT

The player is waiting to hit the ball on the count of "five".

STAGE 3
Contact point

Meet the ball as you reach "five" on your timing count. Make sure that you stop on the ball.

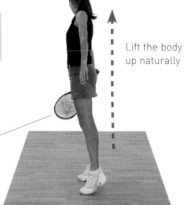

Lift the body up naturally

Stop the racket on the ball

FROM THE BACK

As the player hits down with the open racket face, notice the body lifting naturally.

The non-dominant arm stays behind

FROM THE RIGHT

The player stops the racket on the ball. The racket face is more open than with a high volley.

The upper body unwinds naturally

FROM THE LEFT

The player has adopted a closed stance. Let your feet move naturally to the ball.

LOW BACKHAND VOLLEY • STAGES 2&3

Straighten the arm as you make contact

The player is intently watching the ball as contact is made.

FROM THE FRONT

MANTRA
Stop on the ball

STAGE ONE

STAGE TWO

STAGE THREE

STAGE FOUR

Backhand half volley

There will be times, when you are close to the net, when the ball will hit the floor before you hit it. This may be due to the ball coming right at your feet. Because you have so little time to react, you will have to lift the ball as soon as it has hit the floor, using the half volley.

THE ESSENCE OF THE SHOT

React quickly to lift the ball as soon as it hits the court.

Lift the ball

Lift the body

STAGE 3
Contact point

Get down to the ball with the racket face slightly closed in order to cover the ball as you lift it.

Most of your weight is on the front foot

Get down to the ball

FROM THE BACK

The player's body weight is mostly on his front foot.

The non-dominant arm aids balance

Keep your head still

FROM THE RIGHT

The contact point here is close to the foot.

 FROM THE LEFT

The player reaches comfortably down to the ball.

Lift the body naturally

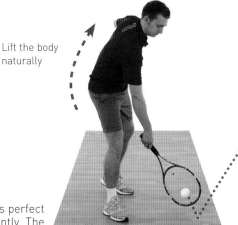

STAGE 4
The finish

Allow your body to lift naturally with the shot.

The angle of the racket is perfect to lift the ball efficiently. The player's head is still while watching the ball.

FROM THE FRONT

returns of serve

RETURN 1

RETURN 2

RETURN 3

RETURN 4

RETURN 5

Returns of serve

The serve and return of serve are the most important shots in the game. Should you not be consistent in either of these areas, your game will suffer. How these two shots are delivered will normally determine the outcome of the point.

Timing
All successful strokes in tennis rely on efficient timing, which involves counting from one to five fairly quickly when "waiting" for the ball. Count "one" on the bounce and hit the ball on "five". As your opponent hits the ball, take a small split step, track the ball and move accordingly.

Spin
When returning, hit either topspin or slice.

The essence of the shots
Your aim is to return your opponent's serve and prevent them gaining an advantage on their service game, thereby giving yourself a level playing field and a chance to break their serve.

Grip
Use the grip that is necessary for the type of shot you want to play (see pages 13–15).

STAGE 1
Get ready

With all types of service returns, you must adopt an alert ready position.

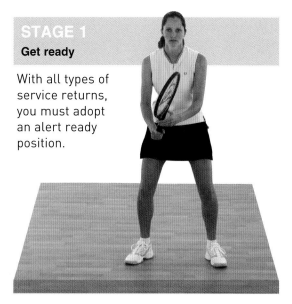

RETURN 1

Topspin forehand

This shot is struck in a similar way to the forehand topspin (see pages 16–23). You may have less time to strike the ball; therefore your backswing becomes shorter accordingly.

Keep your forearm slightly flexed

FROM THE BACK

The player adopts an open stance and places her body weight to the side she is hitting.

Use your triceps and biceps to pull the racket upwards

The wrist is laid off

FROM THE RIGHT

The contact point is in front of the player.

The player maintains excellent balance due to her open stance.

FROM THE LEFT

Use the squareness of the strings to generate masses of topspin

This hand aids balance

The player watches the ball closely as she makes contact with it.

FROM THE FRONT

RETURN 2
One-handed topspin backhand

This shot is struck in a similar way to the one-handed topspin backhand (see pages 32–37). You may have less time to strike the ball; therefore your backswing becomes shorter accordingly.

Pull the racket head up

FROM THE BACK

The player adopts a closed stance for comfort. If you receive a powerful serve you could adopt an open stance.

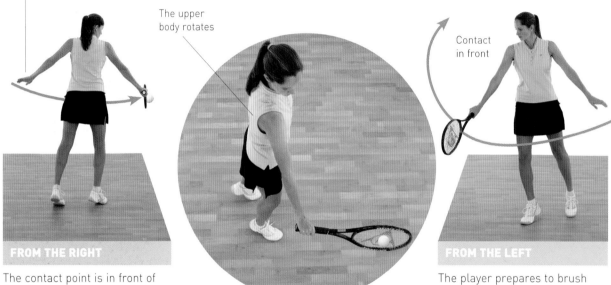

The non-dominant hand aids balance

The upper body rotates

Contact in front

FROM THE RIGHT

The contact point is in front of the player.

FROM THE LEFT

The player prepares to brush up the back of the ball to impart topspin.

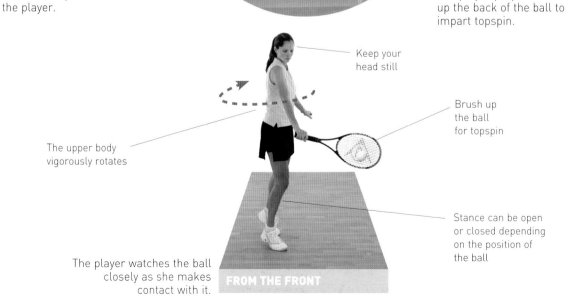

Keep your head still

Brush up the ball for topspin

The upper body vigorously rotates

Stance can be open or closed depending on the position of the ball

The player watches the ball closely as she makes contact with it.

FROM THE FRONT

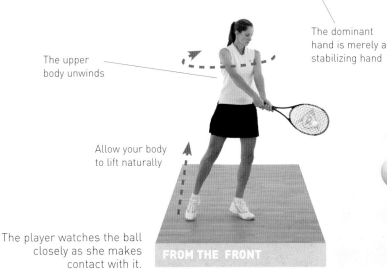

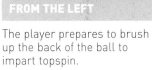

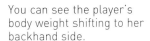

RETURN 3

Two-handed topspin backhand

This shot is struck in a similar way to the two-handed topspin backhand (see pages 24–31). You may have less time to strike the ball; therefore your backswing becomes shorter accordingly.

Open stance

Pull the racket up with your non-dominant hand

FROM THE BACK

The player adopts an open stance. By doing this she can push herself back towards the centre effectively.

FROM THE RIGHT

You can see the player's body weight shifting to her backhand side.

The dominant hand is merely a stabilizing hand

FROM THE LEFT

The player prepares to brush up the back of the ball to impart topspin.

The upper body unwinds

Allow your body to lift naturally

The player watches the ball closely as she makes contact with it.

FROM THE FRONT

MANTRA
Track the ball and count to "five"

RETURNS OF SERVE • RETURNS 2&3

RETURN 4
Forehand slice

This shot is struck in a similar way to the slice forehand (see pages 62–68). You may have less time to strike the ball; therefore your backswing becomes shorter accordingly.

Hit down and across

Keep your wrist laid off

FROM THE BACK

The player adopts a closed stance. She may well be attempting a "chip and charge" tactic.

Keep your head still

Open racket face

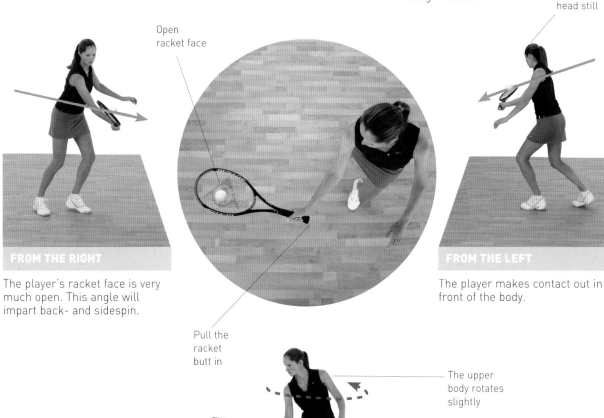

FROM THE RIGHT

The player's racket face is very much open. This angle will impart back- and sidespin.

Pull the racket butt in

FROM THE LEFT

The player makes contact out in front of the body.

The upper body rotates slightly

Stance can be open or closed depending on the position of the ball

The player watches the ball closely as she makes contact with it.

FROM THE FRONT

RETURN 5
Backhand slice

This shot is struck in a similar way to the slice backhand (see pages 38–44). You may have less time to strike the ball; therefore your backswing becomes shorter accordingly.

Hit down and across

Stance can be open or closed depending on the position of the ball

The player adopts a closed stance. She may well be attempting a "chip and charge" tactic.

The non-dominant arm aids balance

FROM THE BACK

FROM THE RIGHT

The player makes contact out in front of the body.

Pull the racket butt in

Keep your wrist laid off

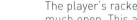

FROM THE LEFT

The player's racket face is very much open. This angle will impart back- and sidespin.

The upper body rotates slightly

The player watches the ball closely as she makes contact with it.

FROM THE FRONT

MANTRA
Track the ball and count to "five"

RETURNS OF SERVE • RETURNS 4 & 5

FOREHAND
topspin lob

FROM ABOVE

FRONT VIEW

RIGHT SIDE

BEHIND

LEFT SIDE

Forehand topspin lob

Should you find yourself at the back of the court, your opponent may choose to attack and advance to the net. Perhaps you hit a ball that landed short. A good counter tactic would be to hit the ball high over your opponent's head with topspin that brings the ball safely down within the confines of the court.

Timing

All successful strokes in tennis rely on efficient timing, when you "wait" for the ball and count from one to five fairly quickly. Count "one" when the ball bounces and brush up the ball on "five".

Topspin

Topspin is essentially when the ball is struck with a brushing-up effect that causes it to rotate vigorously in a forward trajectory.

Grip
The grip normally used for this shot is your chosen forehand grip (see pages 13–14). This is the full western grip.

STAGE 1
Get ready

THE ESSENCE OF THE SHOT

The shot is identical to the forehand topspin (see pages 16–23), except that the ball is lifted higher so that it clears the opponent's head.

Start with the racket in front of you, with your dominant hand in a forehand grip and knees slightly bent.

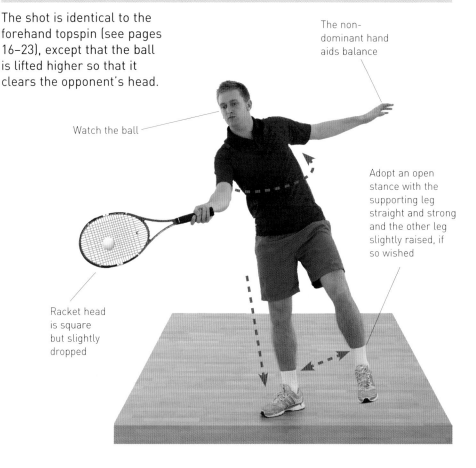

The non-dominant hand aids balance

Watch the ball

Racket head is square but slightly dropped

Adopt an open stance with the supporting leg straight and strong and the other leg slightly raised, if so wished

STAGE 2
Tracking the ball

As you wait for the ball you should also be tracking it, with the racket held in front of you.

Line the ball up with the racket

FROM THE BACK

The racket is supported with both hands, while pointing towards the ball.

Wait for the ball to bounce

FROM THE RIGHT

You can see the racket tilted forwards and supported by the non-dominant hand.

Track the ball with both hands on the racket

FROM THE LEFT

The body leans to the forehand side as the player moves naturally towards the ball.

The upper body starts to rotate

As the player tracks and moves towards the ball, notice that the non-dominant arm is positioned across the body.

FROM THE FRONT

MANTRA
Track the ball

FOREHAND TOPSPIN LOB • STAGES 1&2

STAGE 3
Backswing

Once the ball has bounced, take a backswing, keeping your arm and grip relaxed as you do so.

Take a backswing with the wrist laid off

FROM THE BACK

Notice the racket supported above the hand with the wrist laid off. Also notice the dominant arm flexed and relaxed.

Keep your arm slightly flexed

Keep your head still

FROM THE RIGHT

You can see the racket face angled away from the player, due to the wrist being laid off.

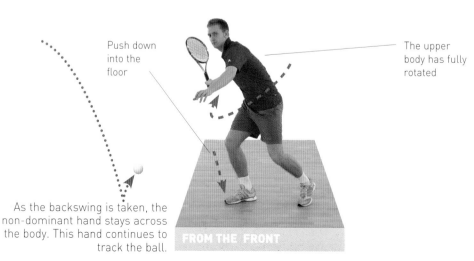

The body weight is pushed down onto the outside leg in an open stance.

FROM THE LEFT

Push down into the floor

The upper body has fully rotated

As the backswing is taken, the non-dominant hand stays across the body. This hand continues to track the ball.

FROM THE FRONT

STAGE 4
Forward swing

As you start the forward swing, drop the racket head and close the racket face. The wrist remains laid off.

The wrist is laid off

Close the racket face

FROM THE BACK

Notice the racket head is now dropped below the hand, with the wrist laid off. The racket face is closed.

Closed racket

Keep your head still

FROM THE RIGHT

The wrist is laid off with the racket butt pointing towards the ball. The racket head is below the hand.

FROM THE LEFT

The body weight remains on the outside leg, but now the body is lifting upwards.

Push down on your outside leg

The upper body starts to unwind

The racket butt points at the ball. The racket face is completely closed and the racket head is dropped.

FROM THE FRONT

FOREHAND TOPSPIN LOB • STAGES 3&4

MANTRA
Close the racket face

STAGE 5
Contact point

Contact is made with the ball via a low-to-high brushing-up effect in order to impart topspin.

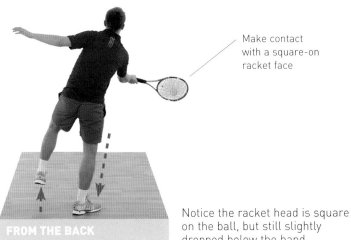

Make contact with a square-on racket face

FROM THE BACK

Notice the racket head is square on the ball, but still slightly dropped below the hand.

Keep your upper body upright

Keep your head still

FROM THE RIGHT

You can see the player is now leaning back, with the weight on the back leg.

FROM THE LEFT

While leaning back, the player can really get under the ball to lift it high.

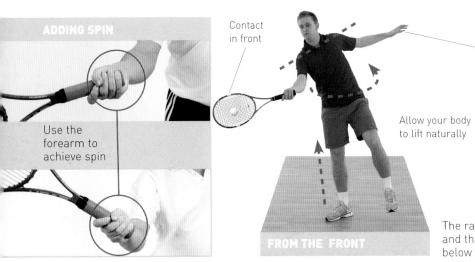

ADDING SPIN

Use the forearm to achieve spin

Contact in front

Use your non-dominant arm for balance

Allow your body to lift naturally

FROM THE FRONT

The racket face is slightly open and the head is slightly dropped below the hand.

STAGE 6
The finish

Finish the forehand topspin lob with your racket over your shoulder.

End the shot with a shoulder finish

FROM THE BACK

Notice the racket head over the shoulder, and the body weight, which is now transferred to the opposite leg to aid recovery.

Racket frame is perpendicular with the shoulder

FROM THE RIGHT

From here you can see the elbow of the dominant arm pointing directly forwards.

Keep watching the ball

The elbow is pointing forwards

FROM THE LEFT

The racket head is over the opposite shoulder and the non-dominant hand is in line with the cheek.

The upper body has fully unwound

You can see the racket butt and elbow pointing forwards. The player still watches the ball, anticipating the next shot.

FROM THE FRONT

FOREHAND TOPSPIN LOB • STAGES 5&6

MANTRA
Get it over your opponent's head

BACKHAND **topspin lob**

FROM ABOVE

FRONT VIEW

RIGHT SIDE

BEHIND

LEFT SIDE

Backhand topspin lob

This backhand shot can be either single- or double-handed. Like the forehand topspin lob (see pages 100–107), you can play this shot when your opponent advances to the net.

Timing

All successful strokes in tennis rely on efficient timing. When "waiting" for the ball count from one to five fairly quickly. Count "one" when the ball hits the floor and "five" when you strike it.

Topspin

Topspin is essentially when the ball is struck with a brushing-up effect that causes it to rotate vigorously in a forward trajectory. This causes the ball to dip and land safely in the court.

Grips
Use either a one-handed or two-handed backhand grip (see page 15).

THE ESSENCE OF THE SHOT	STAGE 1 **Get ready**

Make sure you accelerate up the back of the ball and get plenty of height.

Brush up for topspin

Stand in the ready position with the racket in front. The example used here is of a two-handed backhand lob.

STAGE 2
Tracking the ball

Track the ball as it comes towards you by lining it up with the racket held in front of you.

The upper body starts to rotate

Track the ball by lining it up with the racket

Notice how the racket is tracking the ball in front of the player on the backhand side.

FROM THE BACK

Keep your head still

FROM THE RIGHT

From here you can see the body weight starting to shift to the backhand side.

FROM THE LEFT

Notice how the racket is tracking slightly in front of the player, with both hands on the grip.

1-HANDED FROM THE FRONT

Body weight shifts to the backhand side as the player tracks the ball in front.

Wrists are laid off

FROM THE FRONT

ADDING SPIN

Use the forearms to achieve spin

STAGE 3
Backswing

As the ball bounces, take a backswing with the time you have available. Make sure your non-dominant hand drives the racket.

Take a backswing

FROM THE BACK

Notice how the upper body has naturally turned during the backswing, and that the player pushes down into the floor.

FROM THE RIGHT

You can either be in an open or closed stance, depending on the position of the ball.

Push down in open stance

The player's eyes are on the ball, focusing on the timing and spin of the shot.

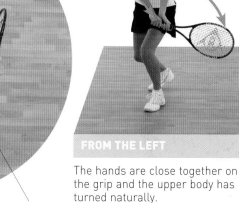

FROM THE LEFT

The hands are close together on the grip and the upper body has turned naturally.

The racket butt is pointing at the ball

1-HANDED FROM THE FRONT

FROM THE FRONT

MANTRA
Track the ball

BACKHAND TOPSPIN LOB • STAGES 2&3

STAGE 4
Back stance

As you swing forwards, drop back into back stance while lifting the ball.

Drop the racket head before brushing up the back of the ball

Notice how the racket has dropped prior to acceleration up the back of the ball, to get lift and spin.

FROM THE BACK

Keep your back upright

Keep your head still

FROM THE RIGHT

The weight is clearly on the player's back foot as they prepare to lift the ball.

Work the non-dominant hand

FROM THE LEFT

Notice how open the racket face is in order to lift the ball high over the opponent's head.

Allow your body to lift naturally

1-HANDED FROM THE FRONT

FROM THE FRONT

At this point the player is about to accelerate the racket head up the back of the ball for topspin.

STAGE 5

The finish

After brushing up the ball, pull the racket head up over the opposite shoulder with the non-dominant hand.

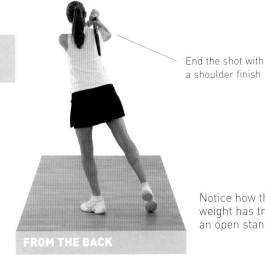

End the shot with a shoulder finish

Notice how the player's body weight has transferred back to an open stance during the finish.

FROM THE BACK

The racket frame is perpendicular with the shoulder

FROM THE RIGHT

FROM THE LEFT

You can clearly see the body weight now transferred to an open stance as the player finishes the shot.

The elbows are off the chest and pointing forwards.

The player has finished the shot over the shoulder, but still watches the ball, anticipating the next shot.

1-HANDED FROM THE FRONT

FROM THE FRONT

MANTRA
Always finish

BACKHAND TOPSPIN LOB • STAGES 4&5

forehand smash

FROM ABOVE

FRONT VIEW

RIGHT SIDE

BEHIND

LEFT SIDE

Forehand smash

Should you be at the net and find yourself on the receiving end of a lob, then it may be possible to track the ball and hit down with a powerful smash.

Timing
To help your timing, you need to track the ball with your non-dominant hand, as if you were going to catch the ball.

Grip
The continental grip is normally used for this shot (see page 13).

THE ESSENCE OF THE SHOT	STAGE 1 Get ready

As the ball rises, track it with your non-dominant hand and hit down powerfully.

Hit down with force

Stand in the ready position with the racket in front.

THE STROKES

STAGE 2
Bringing both hands up together

As the ball is lobbed up, start tracking it by raising both hands together.

Bring both arms up together

FROM THE BACK

The non-dominant hand is pointing up at the ball; the racket arm is bent behind the head.

Elbows are aligned

Track and watch the ball

FROM THE RIGHT

Notice the straight line passing from the extended arm into the racket arm.

FROM THE LEFT

Notice the tip of the racket head pointing at the ball.

Turn side on

Keep your head still

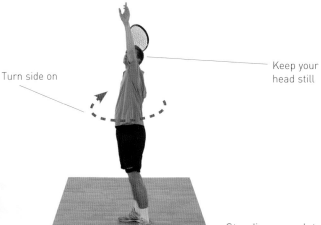

FROM THE FRONT

MANTRA
Bring both hands up together

Standing completely sideways on as you track the ball will help you balance when it's time to move.

STAGE 3
Contact point – reaching upwards

Reach up to smash the ball downwards. Sometimes you may come off the floor.

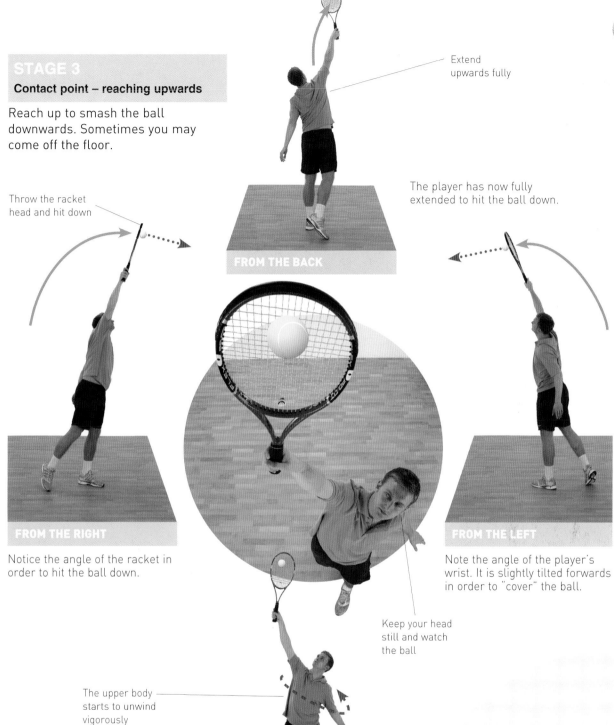

Extend upwards fully

The player has now fully extended to hit the ball down.

FROM THE BACK

Throw the racket head and hit down

FROM THE RIGHT

Notice the angle of the racket in order to hit the ball down.

FROM THE LEFT

Note the angle of the player's wrist. It is slightly tilted forwards in order to "cover" the ball.

Keep your head still and watch the ball

The upper body starts to unwind vigorously

Watch the ball as you reach up to hit down.

FROM THE FRONT

FOREHAND SMASH • STAGES 2 & 3

MANTRA
Reach up

STAGE 4

Snapping the wrist

As the player hits down on the ball, you can see the downward snapping of the wrist.

FROM THE BACK

The player has snapped down on the ball.

Snap the wrist

FROM THE RIGHT

Hit down to get power.

FROM THE LEFT

As the player snaps down on the ball, the arm stays relaxed.

The upper body has fully unwound

The non-dominant hand aids balance

MANTRA
Snap down
on the ball

FROM THE FRONT

The player continues to watch the ball.

STAGE 5
The finish

After the smash, the racket tends to finish around the opposite side, at about waist height.

Racket at waist height

FROM THE BACK

Note the racket head finishing around the player's opposite side, at about waist height.

The racket frame is perpendicular with the floor

FROM THE RIGHT

The player has elected to step forwards, maybe to move back into the net.

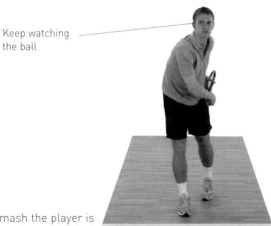

FROM THE LEFT

You can clearly see the player's racket finish as he advances down the court.

Keep watching the ball

FROM THE FRONT

After the smash the player is always alert and ready to deal with the next shot.

MANTRA
Get ready for the next shot

FOREHAND SMASH • STAGES 4&5

backhand smash

FROM ABOVE

FRONT VIEW

RIGHT SIDE

BEHIND

LEFT SIDE

Backhand smash

Only hit this shot if you don't have time to move around to hit a forehand smash (see pages 114–119).

Timing
To help your timing, track the ball by pointing your racket butt at it.

Grip
The continental grip is normally used for this shot (see page 13).

STAGE 1
Get ready

THE ESSENCE OF THE SHOT

As the ball rises, track it with your racket butt and hit down powerfully.

Stand in the ready position with the racket in front.

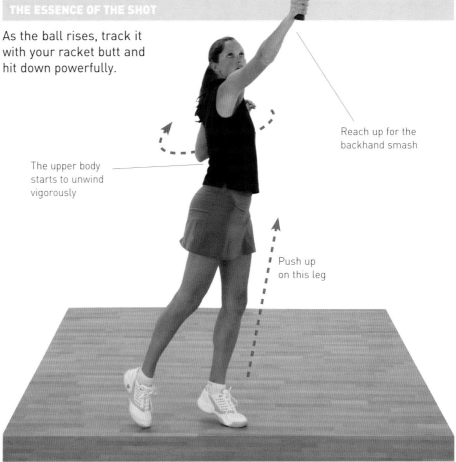

The upper body starts to unwind vigorously

Reach up for the backhand smash

Push up on this leg

Point the racket butt at the ball

STAGE 2
Tracking the ball

As the ball is lobbed up, start tracking it by pointing the racket butt at the ball.

FROM THE BACK

The non-dominant hand supports the throat of the racket as the player tracks the ball.

The racket face is completely open

Keep your head still

FROM THE RIGHT

The body weight leans to the backhand side, with the elbow pointing upwards.

FROM THE LEFT

You can clearly see the racket butt pointing upwards.

BACKHAND SMASH • STAGES 1&2

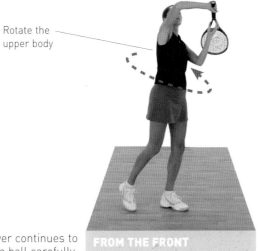

Rotate the upper body

The player continues to watch the ball carefully.

FROM THE FRONT

MANTRA
Point the racket butt

THE STROKES

STAGE 3

Contact point – reaching upwards

Reach up to smash the ball downwards.

Fully extend upwards

The player has now fully extended to hit the ball down.

FROM THE BACK

Hit the ball above the racket centre

Keep your head still

FROM THE RIGHT

Notice the angle of the racket in order to hit the ball down.

FROM THE LEFT

Note the angle of the player's wrist. It is slightly tilted forwards in order to "cover" the ball.

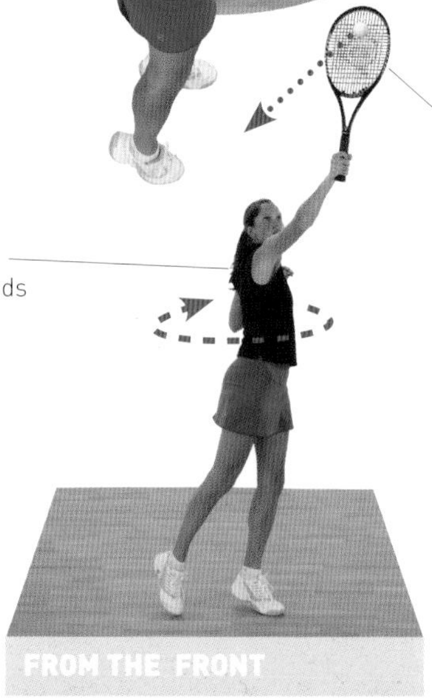

The upper body unwinds vigorously

Pull the racket head down

MANTRA
Reach up

FROM THE FRONT

Watch the ball as you reach up to hit down.

STAGE 4
The finish

As you smash, squeeze your shoulder blades together to obtain power.

Squeeze the shoulders together

You can see the player has hit down and across the ball, and her shoulder blades are now squeezed together.

FROM THE RIGHT

You can clearly see the player's shoulders pulling back.

Keep watching the ball

FROM THE LEFT

Notice the position of the player's racket once she has hit down and across.

Pull down and across

The body has fully unwound

After the smash the player is continually watching the ball to anticipate the next shot.

FROM THE FRONT

MANTRA
Squeeze your shoulders; hit down and across

BACKHAND SMASH • STAGES 3 & 4

FOREHAND
drive volley

FROM ABOVE

FRONT VIEW

RIGHT SIDE

BEHIND

LEFT SIDE

Forehand drive volley

This shot is played when a player is advancing from the baseline to take the ball out of the air before it bounces with a topspin contact. It is highly aggressive and can be used on both the forehand and backhand side.

Timing
Count "one" on the opponent's contact and hit the ball on the count of "five".

Grip
Use the grip that you would normally use for a topspin forehand (see page 18). This is a semi-western grip.

THE ESSENCE OF THE SHOT

As the ball rises, track the ball and take it out of the air with a topspin contact.

STAGE 1
Get ready

Stand in the ready position with the racket in front.

STAGE 2
Tracking the ball

Track the ball at the relevant height, in this case shoulder height, with the racket held in front of you.

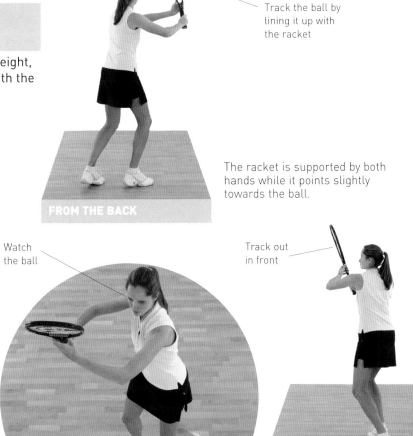

Track the ball by lining it up with the racket

FROM THE BACK

The racket is supported by both hands while it points slightly towards the ball.

Flex your elbow

Watch the ball

Track out in front

FROM THE RIGHT

The racket is tilted forwards as the ball is tracked while being supported by the non-dominant hand.

FROM THE LEFT

The body leans to the forehand side as the player moves naturally towards the ball.

The upper body starts to rotate

As the player tracks and moves towards the ball, the non-dominant arm is positioned across the body.

FROM THE FRONT

STAGE 3
Backswing

The player counts "one" as her opponent hits the ball. She then takes a backswing, keeping the arm and grip relaxed.

The racket face is turned away

The wrist stays laid off

FROM THE BACK

The racket is supported above the hand with the wrist laid off. The dominant arm is flexed and relaxed.

Keep the arm flexed

FROM THE RIGHT

The racket face is angled away from the player due to the wrist being laid off.

FROM THE LEFT

The body weight is pushed down onto the outside leg in an open stance.

The upper body has fully rotated

Open stance

As the backswing is taken, the non-dominant hand stays across the body and continues to track the ball.

FROM THE FRONT

MANTRA
Track the ball

FOREHAND DRIVE VOLLEY • STAGES 2&3

STAGE 4
Contact point

Contact shown here is at shoulder height. Contact is made with the ball via a low-to-high brushing-up effect in order to impart topspin.

The racket face is square

FROM THE BACK

The racket head is square on the ball but the head is only slightly dropped below the hand.

Pull up and across the ball

Keep your head still

FROM THE RIGHT

The contact point is comfortably in front with the elbow flexed. The racket head will now accelerate upwards.

FROM THE LEFT

The body has pushed up and the stance remains open.

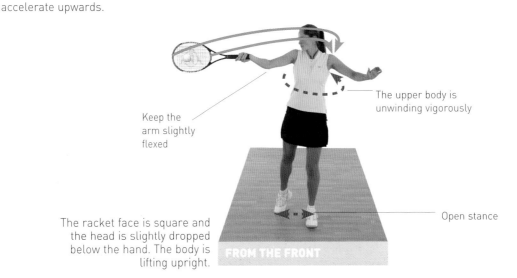

Keep the arm slightly flexed

The upper body is unwinding vigorously

Open stance

The racket face is square and the head is slightly dropped below the hand. The body is lifting upright.

FROM THE FRONT

STAGE 5

The finish

As you pull across the ball, finish over your shoulder.

The shoulder finish

The racket frame is perpendicular with the floor

The racket head is over the shoulder, with the body weight transferred to the opposite leg to aid recovery.

FROM THE BACK

FROM THE RIGHT

The elbow of the dominant arm points directly forwards.

Keep watching the ball

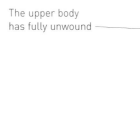

FROM THE LEFT

The racket head is over the opposite shoulder, and the non-dominant hand is in line with the cheek.

The upper body has fully unwound

FROM THE FRONT

The racket butt and elbow point forwards. The player still watches the ball, anticipating the next shot.

FOREHAND DRIVE VOLLEY • STAGES 4&5

MANTRA
Always finish the shot

ONE-HANDED BACKHAND
drive volley

FROM ABOVE

FRONT VIEW

RIGHT SIDE

BEHIND

LEFT SIDE

One-handed backhand drive volley

This shot is played when a player is advancing from the baseline to take the ball out of the air before it bounces with a topspin contact. It is highly aggressive and can be used on both the forehand and backhand side.

Timing

Count "one" on the opponent's contact and hit the ball on the count of "five".

Grip

Use the grip that you would normally use for a topspin backhand (see page 33).

(see page 33)

THE ESSENCE OF THE SHOT

As the ball rises, track the ball and take it out of the air with a topspin contact.

Keep your head still

The upper body has fully unwound

Pull across the ball

STAGE 1

Tracking the ball

Find your grip and track the ball by pointing the racket butt towards it.

Point the racket butt

STAGE 2
Contact point

After counting "one" to "five," pull up and across the ball when you reach "five".

Pull up and across the back of the ball

FROM THE BACK

The non-dominant hand is released and the racket head is level with the player's hand.

FROM THE RIGHT

The player lifts his body as he makes contact with the ball in front.

FROM THE LEFT

At contact point, the racket face is square against the ball.

The player watches the ball intently as he pulls the strings across the ball.

FROM THE FRONT

STAGE 3
The finish

After pulling across the ball, the racket head finishes across the body. The shoulder blades are squeezed together for power output.

The "shoulder blade squeeze" finish

The player's shoulder blades have squeezed together for power output.

FROM THE BACK

Keep watching the ball

FROM THE RIGHT

Both arms pull back behind the player.

FROM THE LEFT

The racket finishes in an upright position, out to the side.

The upper body has completely unwound

The player has finished the shot but he still watches the ball, anticipating the next shot.

FROM THE FRONT

ONE-HANDED BACKHAND DRIVE VOLLEY • STAGES 2&3

MANTRA
Squeeze the shoulder blades together

TWO-HANDED BACKHAND
drive volley

FROM ABOVE

FRONT VIEW

RIGHT SIDE

BEHIND

LEFT SIDE

Two-handed backhand drive volley

If you tend to play with a two-handed backhand, you'll probably prefer to use both hands on your drive volley. As with the one-handed forehand and backhand drive volleys (see pages 126–135), this shot is played when a player is advancing from the baseline to take the ball out of the air before it bounces with a topspin contact. It is highly aggressive.

Timing
Count "one" on the opponent's contact and hit the ball on the count of "five".

Grip
Use the grip that you would normally use for a two-handed topspin backhand (see page 26).

THE ESSENCE OF THE SHOT

As the ball rises, track the ball and take it out of the air with a topspin contact.

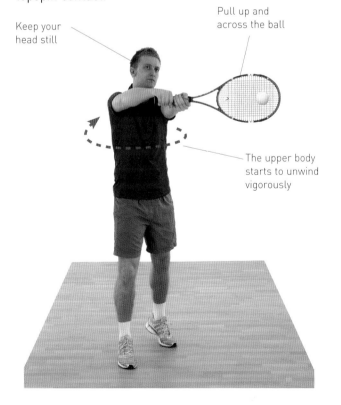

Keep your head still

Pull up and across the ball

The upper body starts to unwind vigorously

STAGE 1
Tracking the ball

Track the ball by lining it up with the racket in front of the body.

The upper body has rotated

STAGE 2
Contact point

Contact is made on count "five" by pulling across the ball in mid-air.

Pull across the ball

The racket head remains slightly below the hands on contact as the player pulls the racket head across.

FROM THE BACK

Keep your head still

Push up from your front foot

FROM THE RIGHT

The player lifts his body as he makes contact with the ball in front.

The racket face is just about level with the hands.

FROM THE LEFT

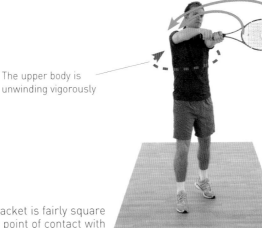

The upper body is unwinding vigorously

The racket face is square on contact

The racket is fairly square at the point of contact with the ball. The strings are pulling across the ball.

FROM THE FRONT

STAGE 3
The finish

After pulling across the ball, the racket head is pulled up over the opposite shoulder with the non-dominant hand.

The shoulder finish

FROM THE BACK

The player's body weight has now transferred back to the opposite side.

Keep watching the ball

FROM THE RIGHT

As the racket has finished over the shoulder, notice how the elbows are off the chest and pointing forwards.

FROM THE LEFT

The racket ends up over the shoulder as the player finishes the shot.

The upper body has fully unwound

The player has finished the shot over his shoulder, but he still watches the ball, anticipating the next shot.

FROM THE FRONT

MANTRA
Always finish

TWO-HANDED BACKHAND DRIVE VOLLEY • STAGES 2&3

learning the ropes

Tennis is a great way to improve your fitness and it's a sociable sport too. It's also an easy one to start, with only a few simple basics — such as clothing, equipment, scoring, rules and court etiquette — to get to grips with.

Jelena Jankovic of Serbia makes an athletic lunge for a wide forehand.

Getting started

You don't need to break the bank to start playing tennis, but there are a few essentials required for practical reasons, and a few items that will help make you feel comfortable on court.

Tennis balls

Always play with good-quality tennis balls. After a while balls will go flat, but do not be tempted to continue playing with them. Playing with flat balls can cause tennis elbow, which is a very painful condition, while rallying with these balls will not help your game. Either throw them away or give them to the dog.

Clothing

Tennis clothes should be loose fitting and made from lightweight material. Polo shirts, T-shirts or vests are ideal. Shorts can be worn by either sex, while female players also have the option of wearing a tennis skirt or a one-piece tennis dress.

Socks should be made of cotton towelling to absorb sweat and aid cushioning of the feet.

At the beginning of a session a track suit or sweatshirt should be worn until the muscles warm up, and don't forget to warm up and stretch properly before you play and to cool down when you have finished playing.

Dress code

Some private tennis clubs have strict dress codes, so make sure you find out what these are before turning up on court.

Keep your hair out of the way with a hairband

Graphite-compound racket is strong yet light to play with

One-piece tennis dress is a comfortable option

Serena Williams, US, world number one.

Quality tennis shoes will have adequate cushioning

Rackets and racket bags

There are many good brands of racket on the market today, including different sizes for juniors. Sizes start at 53cm (21in) for 4 to 5 year-olds and progress up to 69cm (27in) for adults. The size of racket you choose is decided on individual feel and comfort.

Grips are available in different sizes too. For advice on the size of grip you require consult a professional coach or a quality tennis shop. Should your current grip become worn or too small, you can easily buy replacement grips or overgrips.

When you first start playing, one racket is ideal, but as you play more and start to hit the ball harder as you improve, you will need to invest in another identical racket, ensuring that if one racket breaks during a match you have a replacement on standby. Top players can have up to eight rackets, although they usually have a sponsorship deal and therefore don't have to pay for them. Broken strings can be restrung by most coaches or tennis shops.

Investing in a decent-sized racket bag is also a good idea, enabling you to carry all your equipment in one bag.

Protection from sun and heat

During hot, sunny weather it is highly recommended that you protect yourself with a baseball cap, sport sunglasses, sweatbands and sunscreen, and that you towel yourself down at regular intervals. Drink plenty of fluids to keep yourself hydrated.

Shoes

Good tennis shoes must be worn. These should include adequate cushioning and support your feet and ankles when you run and pivot. Ankle supports provide additional stability if needed.

The shoe's grip must be suitable for the surface you will be playing on. Most tennis shoes have a lightweight rubber sole and rubber zigzag grip, although specialist shoes designed for playing on an indoor carpet have a completely smooth sole.

Durable racket strings set at the correct tension

Keep the sun out of your eyes and off your head with a light-coloured cap

Clean, undamaged overgrip

Loose-fitting polo shirt and shorts aid ease of movement

Andy Roddick, US, former world number one.

Ankle supports provide additional stability

REMEMBER
Be prepared

Scoring

Tennis scoring is broken down into matches, sets, games and points.
A set consists of a specified number of games, while to win the match
the player must win a particular number of sets.

Matches

To win a whole tennis match, you
would normally have to win the best
of three sets. However, during grand-
slam events such as Wimbledon, the
Australian Open, the US Open and the
French Open, the men play the best of
five sets.

If you are a recreational player, you
can play as few or as many sets as
you like.

Games and points

To win a game, a player has to win
four points (except in the case of
deuce). Both players start off with zero,
or "love". The first point takes the player
to 15, the second point to 30, the third
to 40 and the next point is "game".

However, if the score reaches 40–40
it is "deuce". From here a player needs
to win by two clear points — taking him
to "advantage" and then "game". If the
player with the advantage loses the
next point, the score reverts to deuce.
The score can seesaw back and forth
until a player wins the next point after
their advantage.

Play changes ends after every odd
number of games. For example, if the
score was 3–2 you would change ends,
but you would stay put at 2–2.

Sets

To win a set, a player has to win six
games, although they also have to win
the set by at least two clear games.
Therefore, if the score is five games
all during a set, play continues until a
player has won 7–5.

If the score reaches 6–6, a tiebreak
must be played. The first player to
reach seven points wins the tiebreak.
However, the player has to win by two
clear points. If the tiebreak score is
six points all, then play continues until
one player is two clear points in front.
During a tiebreak, players change ends
every six points played.

In a professional tournament,
if the players are playing the last set
in a match, they might have to play
a long set. This means there is no
tiebreak in the last set, therefore play
continues until a player has won by
two clear games.

Whilst you may have to keep
a mental tally of the score,
professionals enjoy the luxury
of large, electronic scoreboards.

Point calling

When calling out the point score, the server's score is always called first, no matter what their score is. For example, if player A serves and wins the point against player B, the score is called out "15–love". If player B wins the point the score is called "love–15".

If at any time the point score is equal with both players on 15 or 30 each, the score is called "15 all" or "30 all". If the score reaches a tie at 40–40, "deuce" is called. If player A wins the next point the score is called "advantage player A". Should player A win the next point as well they would win that game. However, if player B wins that point the score would revert back to deuce.

Justine Henin challenges a call at Wimbledon by using Hawk-Eye, the virtual reality system used in many tournaments.

REMEMBER
Learn the intricacies of scoring by playing the game

Serving and rallying rules

The serve, return of serve and any ensuing rally are the point-scoring opportunities of a game. As such, it's important to be absolutely clear on how these points can be played out.

Serving

The very first point of a game is served from the right side of the court. The player stands behind the baseline and serves diagonally, so that the ball bounces in the opponent's service box.

If the serve lands outside the service box, or hits the net and does not go over, "fault" is called and the server is allowed another attempt, called a "second serve". However, should the player miss this serve as well, "double fault" is called and the point is awarded to the returner. The server will also fault if one or both of their feet touch or cross the baseline before they strike the serve. This is known as a "foot fault".

Should a serve strike the top of the net but still go over and into the correct service box, "net" is called and the server will attempt another serve but will not be faulted. This is known as a "first serve". The player can keep doing this many times and never be faulted. However, should the serve hit the net and land outside the service box, the server will be faulted as normal. Should the ball hit the net during a rally, however, the players must play on.

Rallying

Following a successful serve, the opponent must attempt to return the ball over the net after one bounce and land it within the confines of the singles court. The area between the two tramlines is considered "out" for singles (see next page for Doubles rules variations).

After that, each player must respond in the same way. Only one bounce is allowed before a player must hit the ball. However, a player may also hit the ball before the bounce. As a player you must not hit the ball more than once to clear the net; let the ball touch any part of you during the rally; or hit the ball down into your side of the court before it goes over the net.

When a player fails to make a successful return of the ball they concede the point.

A player prepares to serve by bouncing the ball first, aiding focus and composure.

Nicolas Kiefer reaches for a two-handed backhand.

Doubles rules variations

During a doubles match, should you elect to serve the first game, service is passed to one of your opponents to serve the next game, then your partner will serve the next and your second opponent will serve the next. After which time service will revert back to you once again. You must keep to this order throughout the set.

At the start of the next set, you may change the order with your partner if you wish to do so.

When returning, once you have stipulated the side you are returning from, that is the side that you must return from during that set. At the start of the next set you may change with your partner if you wish to do so.

In doubles games the area between the tramlines is considered "in" during a rally but not for the serve.

Completing the game

After the first point is won, the server then serves from the left side and serves diagonally to the opposite service box. Points continue to be played in the same way until one player has won the game, when the returning player will take their turn to serve.

The fastest serve: American Andy Roddick, 249km/h (155mph) against Vladimir Voltchkov of Belarus during the Davis Cup in September 2004.

FACT

Wheelchair tennis

The rules of the International Tennis Federation (ITF) wheelchair sport are the same as above, except that the ball is allowed to bounce twice. The players have specially designed wheelchairs to help them manoeuvre around the court.

Court etiquette

Tennis is a very competitive sport and sometimes emotions and tempers can run high. Try to be as gracious as you can, but don't let your opponent walk all over you by calling every score and overruling your line calls.

Beginning the first game

Spinning the racket is the usual way of deciding who will serve the very first game in the match. Use the knots on the strings as a guide. The side with the knots pointing up is known as the "rough" side, while the opposite side is referred to as the "smooth" side. Other variations can be used, such as the direction of the racket's brand motif.

Ask your opponent to choose a side, then spin the racket. Whoever wins the toss can decide whether to serve first or second, or choose which end to play first, but not both. For example, if you win the toss, you may elect to serve first. Your opponent may then elect which end to start from. This decision can be crucial when playing outdoors. A good choice would be to play into the sun on the first game if possible, due to the fact that you will be playing out of the sun on the next two games.

Line calling

When playing a friendly match or the first few rounds of a tournament, the players are responsible for calling both the score and line calls, because there is no umpire to oversee the match. Normally, you will judge your opponent's shots and they will judge yours. In this instance please try to be as fair as you can. If your opponent's shot lands in, stay silent and simply play the ball back. If you judge the shot as out then you must call it as soon as the ball has bounced, in a clear voice that your opponent can hear.

You each may question each other's line calls, and if you fail to agree you can simply play the point again, although normally the player who has made the initial judgment has the decision to replay or to stand firm, so an element of discretion should be used here.

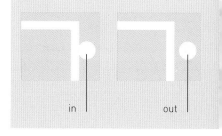

in   out

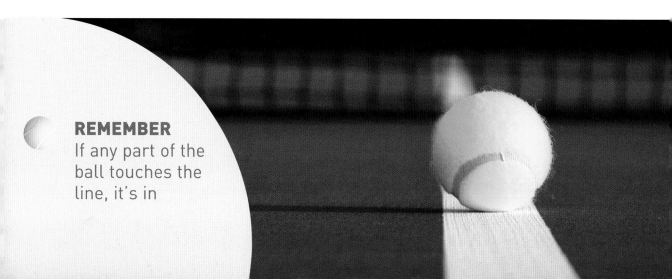

REMEMBER
If any part of the ball touches the line, it's in

Practise good sportsmanship at all times: don't serve until your opponent is ready (when they stand in ready position facing you); at the end of a match always shake hands with your opponent — win or lose — and the umpire, if there is one.

tactics

Keeping some tactical strategies in mind could give you that essential advantage over your opponent. This section covers the critical points of the game and gives you some ideas on how to give your tennis that winning edge.

French player Paul-Henri Mathieu fires himself up after winning a point in the fashion he intended.

Tactical serving

The serve is one of the most important shots in the game. If you don't master it you will hand cheap points to your opponent by double faulting or producing weak serves that asked to be attacked. However, if you can master placement and possess great pace on your serve, you really will be feared.

REMEMBER
Place the ball

Placement

Placing the ball well is the most important aspect of serving. Pace — how hard you hit the ball — is also important, certainly, but learning to place the ball will not only increase your chances of landing it in the service box, but also enable you to serve regularly to your opponent's weaker side, thus forcing them to return weakly, if at all.

However, if you keep serving to one side your opponent will get wise. If you do not possess a powerful serve that will produce a huge number of aces (points won by the serve alone), serving 90 per cent of your serves to your opponent's weaker side is a good idea. You can also serve to the stronger side and at the body of your opponent. Once you learn to place your serves within a few centimetres, you will keep your opponent guessing where you are going to serve next.

The history of tennis shows us that the most successful servers of all time were not necessarily the fastest in their day. Indeed, you can hit your fastest serve into the hitting zone of an opponent and all they have to do is block it back or, worse still, drive it back with topspin. By placing your serve wide and close to the lines, you stand a much better chance of the ball flying right past your helpless opponent, even with a fraction of the pace.

Targets

You can't practise your serve enough, and you don't always need a practice partner. Set up some special collapsible cones as targets in the service box, or just use your jacket, a tin of balls or an empty fizzy drink can.

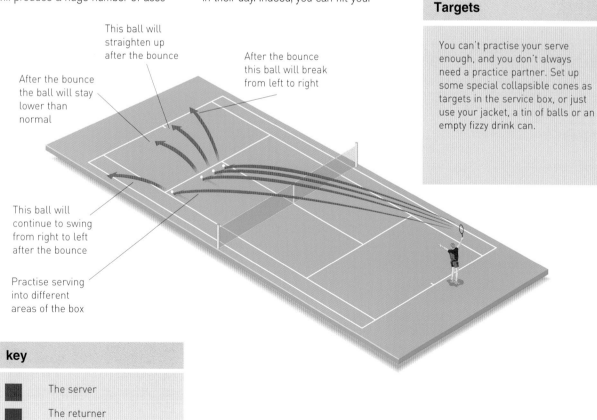

This ball will straighten up after the bounce

After the bounce this ball will break from left to right

After the bounce the ball will stay lower than normal

This ball will continue to swing from right to left after the bounce

Practise serving into different areas of the box

key

■	The server
■	The returner

Four main contacts for the serve

Flat serve

A flat serve is when the ball is hit with very little spin and a lot of power. It is normally used for the first serve only. Many recreational players possess one big flat serve; then if they miss that they simply "plop" their second effort in, which begs to be attacked. Spin serves should be mastered as soon as possible and can be used for both serves.

Hitting a flat serve down the middle of the service box and into the returner's body.

Heavy serve

A heavy serve is used for either a first or second serve. The server slices across the back of the ball as they strike it, imparting a lot of sidespin. Although the trajectory looks straight, like a flat serve, the sidespin causes the ball to "bite" into the strings, making the returner feel that they are hitting a heavy ball.

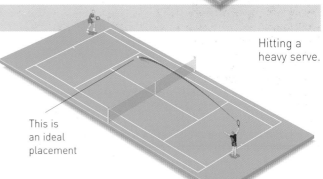

Hitting a heavy serve.

This is an ideal placement

Slice serve

A slice serve can also be used for either a first or second serve. Like the heavy serve, the ball is struck across its surface, only this time more on its side. This again imparts sidespin, but the ball will curve during flight, swinging into or away from the opponent.

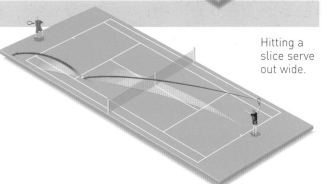

Hitting a slice serve out wide.

Topslice serve

The topslice serve, also known as a topspin serve or American twist serve, is normally used for second serves, although you can use it for a first serve to keep your opponent guessing. The racket strings brush up and across the ball's surface, producing topspin and sidespin. The ball travels up and over the net in a curve, due to the sidespin, but when the ball hits the court, instead of curving away like a normal slice serve, it straightens up due to the topspin, making the serve difficult to read.

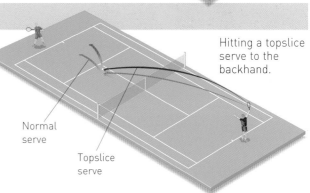

Hitting a topslice serve to the backhand.

Normal serve

Topslice serve

Tactical returning

The return and the serve are equally the most important shots in the game. If you can't get your opponent's serve back you will boost their confidence no end. If your returns are not working you will not get to rally and stand a chance of winning the point.

Defend or attack?

The decision to do one or the other greatly depends on the serve coming at you. If you are facing an aggressive server, your choice should be to defend by standing back behind the baseline and deflecting the ball back.

Should your opponent miss their first serve, or indeed they possess a particularly weak first serve, then you may want to try to be a little more aggressive. You can do this by moving inside the baseline and hitting the ball on the rise (see page 161) and producing more acceleration and topspin on your own shot.

Placement

To ensure total safety, try to hit diagonally across the court – cross court (see page 158) – aiming to land the ball three-quarter length or "deep". This will prevent your opponent gaining an easy attacking opportunity.

You could also try hitting straight down, close to the singles sidelines, known as hitting "down the line" (see page 159). This is a more attacking option and is a higher risk return, but there is nothing wrong with having a go, especially if the serve is slow and short.

Should you be returning against a serve and volleyer (see page 157), your best bet is to either block or topspin the ball, so that it lands inside the service box. As a result the ball will arrive at the feet of the incoming server, forcing them to lift the ball defensively. You will then have a chance to lob or pass your opponent. The harder option is to pass your opponent on either side as they advance after their serve.

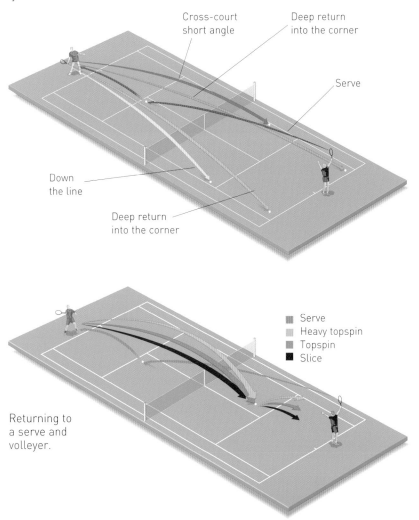

Cross-court
short angle

Deep return
into the corner

Serve

Down
the line

Deep return
into the corner

■ Serve
▒ Heavy topspin
▓ Topspin
■ Slice

Returning to
a serve and
volleyer.

Move in to the net or stay back?

When facing an aggressive server you will most probably end up defending, staying back behind the baseline for the next shot. If you are facing a short first serve, or a second serve that you feel you can attack, you will have a fairly good chance of advancing towards the net. This can put great pressure on your opponent by forcing them into drastic action, such as a lob or a pass. If you are fairly agile and you like to volley and smash, you will have a good chance of winning the point. This is certainly an example of playing to your strengths.

The shot that you play may be topspin or slice, and is classed as an "approach shot", purely because you are approaching the net as you play the ball. Make sure you place your approach shot in such a way as to keep your opponent off balance, for example by hitting to their weaker side.

As you move forwards, keep your eyes on your opponent. As they are about to play their next shot, slow down, because the time is approaching where you may need to suddenly change direction to reach the ball. As your opponent strikes the ball, perform a split step, pushing your feet slightly outwards. This explosive movement will allow you to push off from the balls of your feet in either direction to reach the ball quickly.

Which spin?

You can hit with either slice (back/sidespin) or topspin. Topspin returns are usually struck harder, while slice is normally used for more defensive returns, although you can hit slice just to change pace for the sake of it.

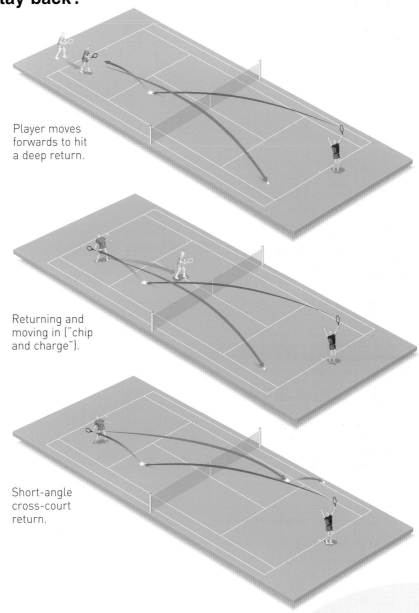

Player moves forwards to hit a deep return.

Returning and moving in ("chip and charge").

Short-angle cross-court return.

key	
■	The server
■	The returner

REMEMBER
Perform the split step before all shots

Tactical first strikes

The first strike is the second shot played by the server, and is just as important as serving and returning. The server would hope that if they haven't won the point on their serve alone (an ace), or an unsuccessful return, then they will have at least forced a weak return of serve that sets them up with a chance to play an attacking shot into the corners. By doing this, if they don't hit an outright winner they can at least force their opponent into an error, known as a "forced error".

Defend or attack?

Whether you defend or attack will depend on the quality of your opponent's return. If your serve possesses sufficient venom, then the chances are that your opponent will return short and allow you to get some purchase on your first strike.

Should your serve be weak, then your opponent will be able to attack it and you may be forced into a defensive or neutral response.

After the first strike

If your opponent hits a short return you may be able to hit a good first strike, then proceed in to the net to put the volley or smash away for a winner.

If net play is not your strong point, you can still hit an attacking first strike and elect to stay back. You can maintain the momentum by bombarding your opponent with aggressive groundstrokes and force them into an error or hit a winner.

Unforced error

An error made while a player is under no real pressure is known as an "unforced error". One of the golden rules of tennis is to keep unforced errors to an absolute minimum.

Rafael Nadal hits a high backhand volley after attacking the net.

Serve and volley

If you have an effective serve and enjoy volleying and smashing, you may elect to serve and volley. This means that once you deliver your serve, you immediately advance to the net, looking for the volley that will deliver that knockout punch. This tactic is very much encouraged in doubles play.

Please note that you must choose to perform this tactic before you serve and stick to your plan. Don't wait to see how your serve pans out because you won't have the time to move in to the net efficiently.

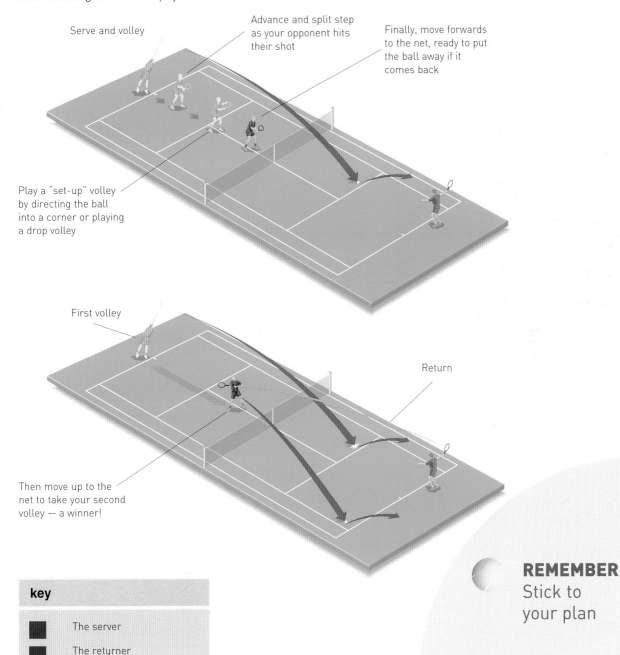

Serve and volley

Advance and split step as your opponent hits their shot

Finally, move forwards to the net, ready to put the ball away if it comes back

Play a "set-up" volley by directing the ball into a corner or playing a drop volley

First volley

Return

Then move up to the net to take your second volley — a winner!

key	
■	The server
■	The returner

REMEMBER
Stick to your plan

Cross court and down the line

As play continues and both players are at the baseline, a number of tactics can come into play.

A forehand or backhand hit diagonally is called a cross-court forehand or backhand, and is a safe shot option because it aims for the largest area of court. Hitting down the line is when the ball runs parallel with the singles line (or doubles line if playing doubles).

If you watch a professional match you will notice that most rallies are exchanged cross court until an opening is created to hit down the line.

Three main cross-court targets

Cross-court centre

Hitting diagonally towards the middle of your opponent's baseline is the safest option because you have plenty of court to aim for and it does not give the opponent a natural angle to hit off. In addition, you are hitting over the lowest part of the net when hitting cross court.

Cross-court corner

Hitting diagonally towards the far corner of the court will make your opponent move wide to the ball, but be aware that if you hit too short you may present your opponent with a natural angle to hit the ball down the line, away from your present position.

Cross-court short angle

Hitting diagonally towards the singles line is the most aggressive angle because it will pull your opponent wide out of court, so if they get the ball back at all it should leave you a nice open court to hit a winning shot. However, it is the higher-risk shot because of the nature of the angle involved: you are hitting to the smallest area of court.

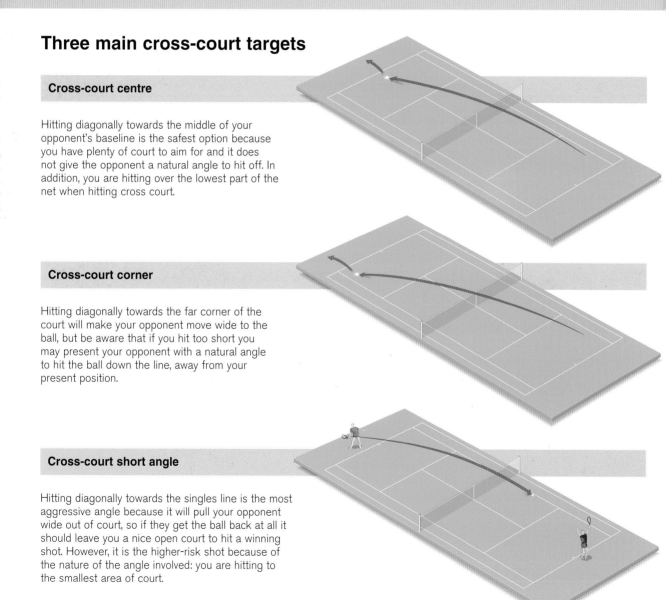

Down the line

Hitting the ball straight down so that it runs parallel with the singles (or doubles) line is slightly more risky in the sense that you have less court to aim for, and probably need to change the direction of a ball that is coming from a cross-court trajectory. You are also hitting over the highest part of the net. However, don't let that put you off, because many players actually develop this shot as their favourite shot, be it a forehand or backhand.

When to do which?

In time, with practice, you will get to know when to play a down-the-line shot as opposed to a cross-court shot. Cross court is the safer option, so you will want to play more of these. It is also harder to change the direction of a fast, deep shot coming at you, so you may want to exchange cross-court blows. However, your aim is to move your opponent around the court, so be patient and wait for a ball that you believe you can hit down the line. If you are playing an opponent who lacks power you will have more opportunities to hit down-the-line shots.

Inside-out/-in forehands

There is nothing wrong with moving around your backhand and hitting a forehand cross-court shot. This is called an "inside-out forehand" (also known as an "off forehand"). Should you choose to hit down the line instead, it is called an "inside-in forehand". You would perform this shot when the ball to your backhand is slow and/or short, so you have time to run around your backhand to hit a forehand. But you must do this for the right reasons. You hit these shots not because you can't hit a backhand but because your forehand is a stronger shot. Watch the top pros and you will see they all use these shots in abundance, and they all have superb backhands.

Roger Federer points the racket butt at the ball before taking a one-handed topspin backhand.

REMEMBER
Play cross court until you can hit down the line

Rallying tactics

Following the service stage of the game, you might find yourself in a rally, exchanging shots with your opponent. Here the point could be won by varying your shots, playing it cool and waiting to exploit one of your opponent's weaker shots or trying to force an error.

Vary pace and spin

During a rally it is always a good idea to change the pace and spin of the ball. This will keep your opponent off balance and deny them any regular timing from your shots. You will find that a lot of errors come off received slower balls, because the player rushes their shot.

Sometimes you will be forced into a change of spin and pace, depending on whether you are attacking, rallying or defending.

Vary height, depth and angle

As well as varying the pace and spin, you should also aim to vary the height of the ball's net clearance. You should ideally aim for 1 metre (4 feet) above net height. By doing this you will achieve consistent net clearance, plus the ball will go deeper.

If you are pushed back behind the baseline by your opponent's shot, hit higher, for the reasons just mentioned, but also to give you time to get back into position. When you hit approach shots, aim for a lower clearance.

Dealing with varying pace, spin and height

Your opponent may be equally good at varying height, pace and spin, in which case you need to watch them very carefully to see how they strike the ball. This will give you an indication of the type of spin being imparted, and therefore the type of bounce to expect. By watching carefully you can also anticipate where they are hitting, how high and at what pace.

Look at the player's body language before, during and after the shot, because this is a clear indicator of the player's comfort and balance and will inform you whether they were able to attack or just able to get the ball back.

Taking the ball on the rise

Taking the ball early means that your opponent has less time to prepare for their next shot, but be careful here. This does not mean you take your racket back earlier; instead it means that you hit the ball as it rises off the floor, known as "taking the ball on the rise".

By doing this you will rush your opponent, giving them less chance to recover from their own shot, plus your shot will be struck harder because the ball still possesses plenty of kinetic energy as it rises off the floor.

Playing the ball from behind the baseline: Rallying

When swapping punches while playing from behind the baseline, try to keep most of your shots cross court, while occasionally hitting down the line (see pages 158–159).

At this point you are looking for weaknesses and waiting for that error, or at least a weak shot, that you can exploit. It is possible to hit a winning shot from here. Keep the ball deep by hitting it at least 1 metre (4 feet) over the net with plenty of topspin.

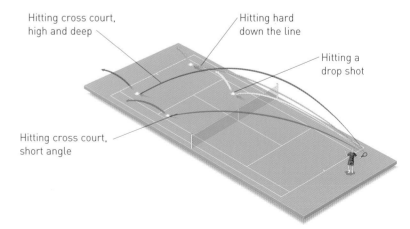

Hitting cross court, high and deep

Hitting hard down the line

Hitting a drop shot

Hitting cross court, short angle

Playing the ball from inside the baseline: Setting up

If you find yourself just inside the baseline you have a number of options open to you. You can try to take the ball on the rise, you can definitely hit more aggressively down the line or you could try a drop shot. Playing inside the baseline gives you a chance to step things up and be creative.

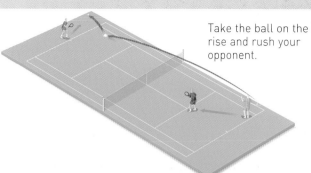

Take the ball on the rise and rush your opponent.

Playing the ball from mid-court: Attacking

When playing the ball from the mid-court area you are on the ascendancy, and should be hitting aggressively into the corners of the court via groundstrokes or even drive volleys. Hit the ball lower over the net as you attack. You are looking to hit a winning shot, or at least a forcing shot that will enable you to put the ball away from inside the service box area, where you should advance to after the shot.

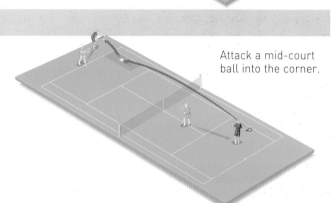

Attack a mid-court ball into the corner.

Playing against a mid-court attack: Defending

If you are on the receiving end of an attack from mid-court, play at the baseline. Aim to counter with passing shots, shots into the body or at the feet and lobs over the head. Your opponent might not be a great volleyer, so don't be afraid to test them by hitting the ball straight at them. Deliberately hit the ball short so that you bring them into a position they are not comfortable with.

If your lob does not clear your opponent's head then you have presented them with a smash opportunity. Realize this early and move right back, further behind the baseline, to defend with more lobs.

Test your opponent with a variety of counter attacks.

Playing the ball from the service box: Finishing

Time for a volley or smash to finish the point. You may also find yourself in this area if you are retrieving a drop shot played by your opponent.

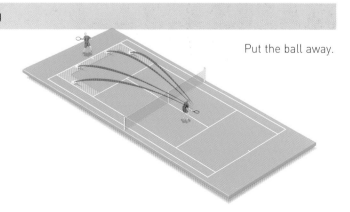

Put the ball away.

20 steps to the right mindset

The most successful professionals are the ones who not only have a skilled game, but also an exceptional ability to stay focused. Whatever level you're playing at, having the right attitude will get you far, and there are certain steps you can follow to maintain it.

1 Be prepared

Develop a pre-match routine that suits you. The night before, try to relax, perhaps by re-watching your favourite classic match or having a hot bath. Always eat a good meal and get a good night's rest.

2 At the court

In general it is a good idea to arrive at the venue early to warm up and have a hit if possible, and to have a light snack and drink before the match. You may even like to listen to music or pre-match instructions on an MP3 player.

3 Learn to play within yourself

Always be ready to step up a gear, but only if you need to. When you watch the best players, they do not always hit their hardest and best shots all the time, but are quite happy to rally and look for opportunities. However, when things get fraught, and they are staring a break point in the face, they step up a gear on their serve as they come up with an ace to get them out of trouble. In other words, you don't have to play your hardest shots all the time. See if you can win points with a fraction of the ability you are capable of, but be ready to play to maximum potential when you really need to.

4 Walk to the back of the court to refocus and plan

Between each point, turn your back on your opponent and walk towards the back of the court. As you do this, start to plan the next rally, and use these precious few seconds to calm and/or towel yourself down, so that when you return to the baseline you are focused and ready to go. This should become one of your rituals.

5 Visualize the rally

As you prepare to serve or return, try to envisage how the rally is going to go, based on previous experience during the match, and consider where you are going to try to hit your first strike.

6 Visualize success before you hit the ball

As you track the ball, visualize the success of the shot in your mind's eye. In other words, picture the spin of the ball as it leaves your racket, and the net clearance of 1 metre (4 feet) or more as it heads in your chosen direction.

7 Congratulate yourself

Give yourself a big pat on the back whenever you achieve a successful shot. By doing this you will attract more of the same. Some players have been known to tap their pocket, as if they are putting the shot in, ready to take out and reuse when they need to. Others clench their fist and shout "come on!" Go on, try it.

8 Play to your strengths

Always hit your favourite shots whenever possible. If you enjoy volleying, then attack the net at every given opportunity. Above all, keep things simple. Play the shots you know you can make most of the time. Occasionally try a more difficult shot, but know your limitations. Know your opponent's strengths and weaknesses too, so that you can isolate their playing style and plan their downfall!

9 Congratulate your opponent

Too many times players go mad when their opponent hits a winner. Your opponent is trying to win the point too, so don't think "how can I have allowed them to hit a winner?" when they are trying to find a way themselves. They are not "lucky", as junior players often proclaim, but skilled, so why not say "good shot"? It makes you feel better, even if you did hit a weak shot that presented them with the opportunity to win the point.

10 Breathe out after you hit

Breathing out just after you hit aids relaxation and releases aggression. Your body must be in a state of full intensity as you meet the ball to produce maximum power, but immediately afterwards you must return to a state of complete relaxation as you breathe out. Some players like to make the exhalation vocal.

11 Be adaptable, not predictable

When you start a match, you should have a plan of how you are going to play this opponent based on previous knowledge and other factors, such as the court surface, weather conditions and so on. But be flexible. If plan A doesn't work, try plan B, and then maybe mix them up. Keep your opponents guessing.

12 Rituals

During your matches it is important to establish rituals to make you feel good. When you are playing, you might tug your shirt or wipe your brow before you serve. These habits could become superstitions, but if you watch the top players, they all have them.

13 Keep your feet moving between points

When you are tense, your feet tend to freeze and become afraid to move, so a little skip between points is useful.

14 Don't be affected by influences beyond your control

You control the way you play, but there are other factors, such as the weather or a bad-tempered opponent who makes poor line calls, that you are unable to control. You simply have to deal with it, and don't use these factors later as excuses for why you lost the match. If you are playing a tournament with a referee you may decide it is necessary to call them over to report your opponent's behaviour. The weather, however, is no excuse, because it is the same for both players. You could even use conditions to your advantage, for example by lowering your ball lift in gusty wind.

15 Maintain your energy levels

Take water and a banana on court, and keep hydrated between end changes. A banana contains potassium that provides a good source of energy.

16 Be patient during points

Don't be in a hurry to finish the point, otherwise you may start rushing shots and making errors. Take your time and enjoy the rally.

17 Revisit your goals

Whatever the result, take the positives out of the match. Did you achieve your goals? These goals could be to take a minimum number of games from a superior opponent or to perform a particular tactic during the match. If you achieved your goals, then well done. Always write your goals down and tick them off as you achieve them.

18 Turn your back on errors

Tennis, for the most part, is a game of errors, not winning shots. So the trick is to make fewer than your opponent. Should you happen to make a few errors, don't over-analyse them or blow a fuse. You will only attract more. Simply turn your back and get ready for the next point.

19 Rehydrate

Don't stop drinking just because you have finished your match. Keep the good stuff flowing, and treat yourself to a snack.

20 Constructive analysis

In the event of a defeat, whatever you do, don't chastise yourself too much, especially directly after the match. Be constructive in all your evaluation.

Doubles tactics and formations

The best doubles pairings in the world know each other and each other's game inside out. They know how to keep their partner motivated when the chips are down, and ways to force opponents to play to their strengths.

The staggered formation and associated tactics

Doubles is essentially a team game. You should understand your partner, be aware of their strengths and weaknesses and, above all, communicate with them throughout the match. Indeed, more experienced doubles players often discuss their strategy before each point, then signal to their serving partners where they want them to serve to and where they personally will move to after the serve goes in. Believe it or not, this can be done with cheeky hand gestures behind the net player's back.

The tramline area is considered "in" for doubles, so the court will seem much wider. However, there is a smaller area for each player to cover.

The essence of doubles play is to get in to the net as soon as possible, but if you are just starting out, playing from the baseline and only coming in to the net upon a short ball from your opponent will be fine.

Staggered (one up, one down) doubles formation

This is the most widely used doubles formation, especially in clubs. The server is positioned behind the baseline, ready to serve, while their partner stands on the opposite side of the court, about halfway up the service box, facing the returner. The returning pair would normally adopt a similar formation. The serving players are treated as the aggressors and the returning pair as the defenders.

The returner stands as far back as they think is necessary to receive the serve. The returner's partner will not be as far forward as the server's partner, but usually around the service line area, due to the fact that they are defending against a possible serve and follow-up volley. This formation is ideal if you are just starting out or if you are an "improver".

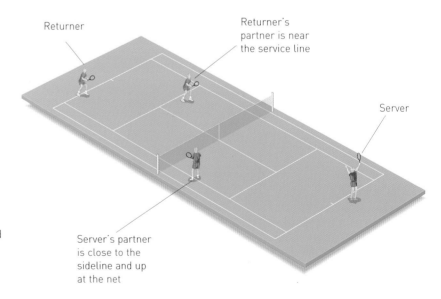

Returner

Returner's partner is near the service line

Server

Server's partner is close to the sideline and up at the net

Serving tactics

Technically, your choice of serve is no different to when playing singles (see page 152). However, because you have a partner, you may serve from a wider position, probably halfway between the centre mark and the singles line.

As with singles play, you must visualize your serve and the likely return. What you want to do, at the very least, is to set your partner up with an easy put-away volley or smash. To this end your placement is essential.

Once you have served, it is a good idea for a beginner player to stay back and rally from the baseline, only moving towards the net when the ball lands short. There are some female professional players who still adopt this tactic, because this is where they feel most comfortable.

As your serve develops into a trusty weapon, and you gain all-round confidence as a player, you should adopt a serve-and-volley tactic (see Serve and volley, page 157). The essence of doubles play is to take control of the net. If you don't, your opponents will. On the whole, good volleyers will defeat good baseliners in doubles because the baseliners have to pass two net players.

The server's partner

When you assume this role, you will be looking to attack weak returns.

First, stand in ready position, roughly halfway between the doubles sideline and the centre line, and halfway up the service box.

As your partner's serve goes in, note the direction and position yourself in line with the ball. By doing this you are attracting the ball, so you can volley it for a winner.

As the returner makes contact, perform a small split step, pushing your feet outwards, so that you are primed to go after the ball, even if the returner directs it cross court. Should this happen, return to your starting position and repeat with every shot from your partner until the ball comes to you or you are able to "poach" (see above).

Poaching/intercepting

"Poaching" is when the net player chooses to nip across to their partner's side of the court to take the volley or smash. This happens in particular when the net player's partner elects to stay back and rally from the baseline.

There are many myths about this tactic at club improver level. It is believed in some quarters to be a "rude" tactic that should be considered a trespass on a partner's patch. However, the golden rule of the staggered formation is that the net player always has first refusal on the ball, which means that poaching, or intercepting, is absolutely the right thing to do.

A player who is willing to take a chance and move to take the ball out is preferable to one who stands still like a rabbit in the headlights. At the same time, however, you don't want a partner who tries to nip across on every other shot, because it is very off-putting and this player is asking to be passed down the tramlines.

So when do you intercept? There is no written rule, but you have to be certain in your own mind that the opponent is going to hit their next shot cross court and you are going to make that shot yours without hesitation. A good pointer as to when to intercept is when you see the opponent struggling to reach the ball, with their body language shaping up to hit a cross-court shot.

Just before your opponent strikes the ball, perform a small split step, push off and move across the court. Hopefully your opponent has committed and is hitting a cross-court shot and you can intercept and finish the volley.

The timing of your move is crucial. Move too early and your opponent will see you, and pass you down the side you have just left. If you move too late the likelihood is that you won't get to the ball in time.

Discuss with your partner before each point when you are going to intercept. You must play as a team.

The server's partner has moved towards the middle of the court, ready to poach.

The returner

When returning, try to identify what kind of player the server is. Are they a baseline player or a serve and volleyer? What kind of first serve do they deliver? Is it a strong serve? Is it attackable? Ask the same questions of the second serve.

Try to place most of your returns cross court, away from the net player. If you present too many opportunities to the net player they should put the ball away. However, every now and then, hit a return at the net player, just to test their net skills and see if they are awake. You'll be surprised.

Should the serve be slow and short, try returning cross court and move in to the net to join your partner in order to finish the point at the net. You could also try a lob return over the server's partner's head.

Should you be facing an aggressive serve-and-volley player, it is a good idea to block or topspin the return down at the feet of the incoming player, so that they have to hit up, presenting you with the opportunity to lob or pass.

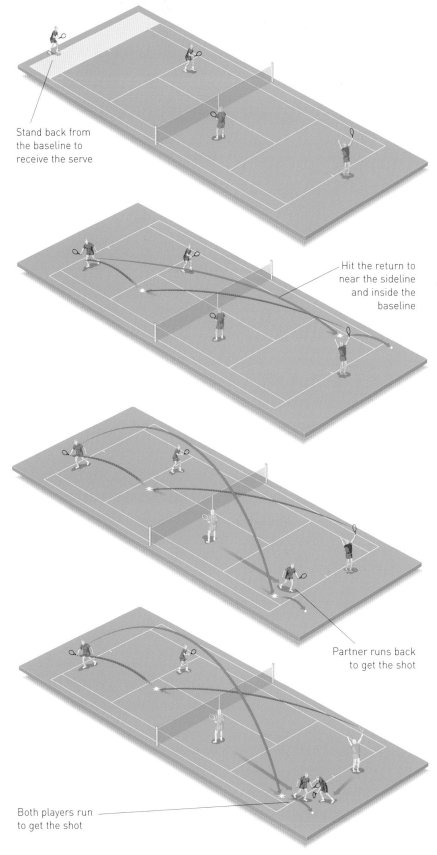

Stand back from the baseline to receive the serve

Hit the return to near the sideline and inside the baseline

Partner runs back to get the shot

Both players run to get the shot

Elena Likhovtseva and Vera Dushevina (foreground) demonstrate the power of the drop shot in a doubles match against Venus Williams and Caroline Wozniacki.

The returner's partner

Start off back on the service line, close to the "T" of the service line, and keep a bird's-eye view on where the serve lands. You have a perfect view and must call it as "out" if you see it so.

Angle your body towards the net opponent. Should your partner hit their return at them then you are perfectly placed to pick up their volley if they hit cross court.

If your partner puts up a short lob and the net player is shaping up for a smash, you must move back quickly, otherwise you might get hit or, worse still, lose the point.

Should your partner hit successfully cross court, move forwards, halfway into the service box and into attack mode. In tennis, defense can turn into counterattack within one shot, and vice versa.

TACTICS

Alternative doubles formations

The following amazing formations are designed to confuse the opponent. Doubles tennis is a game of outwitting your opponents; very much more about placement and touch than sheer power, not least because it is harder to put the ball away when there are two opponents who stand in your way.

"Both at the back" formation

This formation (see below) involves both players at the back. Normally the players would adopt this formation when they are returning. This tactical decision could be due to the fact that they are facing a huge serve and the returns are being picked off by a good volleyer, or purely because one of the players is a little apprehensive about being so close to the net.

The "Australian" formation

This formation is adopted only by the serving pair. The net player, instead of being on the opposite side of the net, is on the same side as the server. It sounds risky for more than one reason, but this formation is used by experienced players who have discussed what is going to happen next before the point actually starts. For example, the returner will see both players on the same side of the court. The returner is then drawn to the huge gap left by the players on the opposite side and may well aim for it. However, this is all part of the ploy. The serving pair is enticing the returner into doing this, so at the last minute one of them nips across, as the serve goes in, to intercept the return of serve with a volley. Cunning, wouldn't you agree?

The "Tandem" or "I" formation

In this formation (right), the server stands very close to the centre mark behind the baseline, while their partner actually crouches down halfway up the centre line that divides the two boxes. Once the serve goes in, the net player has prearranged to jump up and spring left or right. The partner will fill the gap.

Twin brothers Sanchai and Sonchat Ratiwatana of Thailand demonstrate the "I" formation.

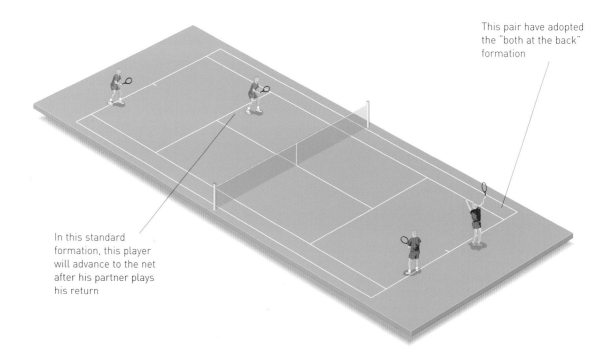

This pair have adopted the "both at the back" formation

In this standard formation, this player will advance to the net after his partner plays his return

TACTICS

The returning player

If you're returning to tennis after a few years' absence, you might find that some of the old ways and rules that were drummed into you by your previous instructor have changed or disappeared altogether. In general, the game has been simplified, and the focus is now on natural physical movement and imparting spin on the ball.

Rotated stance

It used to be taught that you should stand sideways on to the ball, pulling the racket back and waiting for the ball. The focus now is on achieving a continuous, more natural swing, with the racket moving back as the ball bounces and the upper body uncurling as you take the shot, encouraging a quicker response and imparting power.

Square on

You may have been told to step into the ball, regardless of the style of the shot you were receiving or taking, with the racket head aligned with the wrist. Nowadays, the preferred option is to meet the ball square-on, with the arm loose, acting like a whip to increase power. The feet move instinctively to a comfortable position.

Up and across

The "old" position below shows the finish after moving the racket forwards and up to lift the ball on a backhand stroke. This action limits power on the ball. Modern coaches are more inclined to teach hitting up and across the body, fully utilizing the muscles in the back by finishing with a shoulder blade squeeze.

OLD

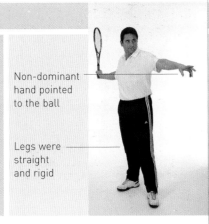

Non-dominant hand pointed to the ball

Legs were straight and rigid

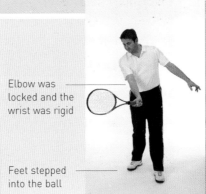

Elbow was locked and the wrist was rigid

Feet stepped into the ball

Power on the ball was limited by forward-and-up arm movement

Players were told to stay low

NEW

Non-dominant arm is across the body

Upper body is rotated

Knees are bent

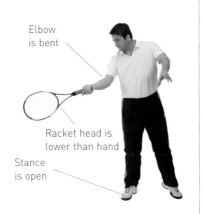

Elbow is bent

Racket head is lower than hand

Stance is open

Arms move behind into a shoulder blade squeeze

Power and spin is gained by hitting up and across

Players are encouraged to lift naturally

Lift up

You may have been advised to stay down at ball level for some strokes. This is a limiting position in which the player had to rely on his arm for providing all the power. It is far more natural, and therefore less likely to cause injury, to use a rotational force, like a spring uncoiling up and into the stroke. In this instance, the player harnesses power from his whole body.

Finishing

With the introduction of slow-motion replay, coaches and players the world over were able to dissect exactly how the pros played. They were fast and dynamic on the court, and advances in graphite racket technology soon demanded even quicker and more fluid game play. Tennis players now have a wealth of finishes to choose from, allowing greater flexibility and more natural, athletic responses. In your own game, you might find that the shoulder finish suits all your needs, but it is always good to have other options at your disposal should you need to respond a little differently to find that winning edge.

OLD

OLD

The racket was caught in front with the non-dominant hand

Body weight was on the front leg, the player having stepped in to meet the ball

With knees bent and body still, the arm had to do all the work.

Shoulder finish: a good beginner's option that can be used for all strokes.

Wrap finish: pulls up and across the ball.

Push down into the floor and lift up to put your whole body behind the shot.

Wiper finish: imparts lots of topspin, whipping short balls up and over the net.

Bullwhip/lasso finish: good for hooking wide balls back into play.

glossary

ACE
A serve that is a winner without the opponent being able to return the ball.

ADVANTAGE
The score for the player who scores following deuce. Should that player win the next point they win the game; should the other player win the score reverts to deuce.

BACKHAND
Stroke performed with the back of the hand facing forwards.

BACKSPIN
Spin of a tennis ball that causes the ball to slow down and/or bounce low.

BACKSWING
Pulling the racket back as the ball bounces. The technique is crucial to timing the ball.

BASELINE
The line indicating the back of the court.

BRUSH UP
The strings contact the ball from low to high, causing the ball to rotate forwards with topspin.

CLOSED RACKET FACE
The racket face is angled downwards.

COCKED WRIST
See *laid off wrist*

CONTINENTAL/HAMMER GRIP
The thumb and index finger straddle the grip from both sides. Normally used for the serve, volley, smash, slice and drop shots.

DEUCE
If the score reaches 40–40. From here a player needs to win by two clear points.

DOUBLE FAULT
When the server misses their second serve and the point is awarded to the opponent.

DRIVE VOLLEY
The player advances from the baseline to take the ball aggressively out of the air before it bounces with a topspin contact.

DROP SHOT
A slice backhand or forehand with an open racket face that causes the ball to drop just on the opposite side of the net.

EASTERN FOREHAND GRIP
Similar to a shaking-hands grip. Normally used for hitting a forehand topspin.

FAULT
When the serve lands outside the opponent's service box or hits the net and does not go over. The server is allowed a second serve.

FIRST SERVE
See *net*

FLAT
A shot with little or no spin.

FOOT FAULT
When one or both of the server's feet touch or cross the baseline before they strike the serve.

FOREHAND
Stroke performed with the palm of the hand turned forwards.

FULL WESTERN GRIP
The hand is almost underneath the racket grip. Normally used to produce large amounts of topspin.

HALF VOLLEY
Lifting the ball as soon as it touches the court.

HAMMER GRIP
See *continental/hammer grip*

HIGH VOLLEY
A volley at head height.

INSIDE-IN FOREHAND
Moving around your backhand and hitting down the line.

INSIDE-OUT FOREHAND
Moving around your backhand and hitting a forehand cross-court shot. Also known as the off forehand.

INTERCEPTING
See *poaching*

LAID IN WRIST
When the wrist is in line with the arm or angled slightly forwards.

LAID OFF WRIST
When the wrist is angled backwards, or "cocked".

LET
See *net*

LOB
Hitting the ball high over the opponent's head with topspin that brings the ball down within the confines of the court.

LOVE
Zero points.

NET/LET
When a serve strikes the top of the net but still goes over and into the opponent's service box. Known as a first serve.

OFF FOREHAND
See *inside-out forehand*

ONE-HANDED TOPSPIN BACKHAND GRIP
The hand is more or less on top of the grip in a bicycle-handlebar-grip fashion.

OPEN RACKET FACE
The racket face is angled upwards.

POACHING/INTERCEPTING
When the net player in doubles chooses to take a volley or smash from their partner's side of the court.

SECOND SERVE
See *fault*

SEMI-WESTERN GRIP
The hand sits just behind the racket grip. The most commonly used forehand topspin grip.

SERVE
The start of every point, this stroke is served from the right side of the court, behind the baseline and diagonally across into the opponent's service box.

SIDESPIN
Makes the ball curve left or right.

SLICE
Striking the ball with sidespin or backspin, or a combination of both.

SMASH
A powerful, downward response to a lob.

SPIN
Rotation of the ball as it moves through the air. Affects trajectory and bounce.

SQUARE RACKET FACE
The racket face is evenly angled toward the ball.

STRIKING THE POSE
Moving to a position that enables the racket to finish up where it should do after the ball is struck.

TIMING
Counting from "one" when the ball hits the floor to "five" when you strike it.

TOPSLICE
When the ball is struck with a combination of top- and sidespin.

TOPSPIN
When the ball is struck with a brushing-up motion that causes it to rotate vigorously in a forward trajectory, causing the ball to dip and land safely in the court.

TRACKING THE BALL
Lining the ball up with the racket in front.

TRAMLINES
The area at both sides of the court that is considered "out" in a singles match and for a doubles serve but "in" for a doubles rally.

TWO-HANDED TOPSPIN BACKHAND GRIP
The non-dominant hand is closer to the throat of the racket in a forehand grip of your choice.

VOLLEY
Returning the ball before it touches the court.

index

Page numbers in italics refer to images

A
analysis: constructive 163
ankle supports 43
"Australian" formation 168

B
backhand:
    one-handed drive volley 132–5
    one-handed drop shot 45
    one-handed slice 38–44
    one-handed topspin 32–7
        grip 15
    two-handed topspin 24–31
        grip 15
backhand half volley 92–3
backhand smash 120–5
    contact point 124
    finish 125
    grip 122
    tracking ball 123
backhand topspin lob 108–13
    back stance 112
    backswing 111
    finish 113
    grip 109
    tracking ball 110
backhand volley:
    contact point 85
    drop 86–7
    low 88–91
        contact point 91
        grip 89
        tracking ball 90
    medium 82–5
        grip 83
        tracking ball 84
ball: tracking 11
balls 142

C
clothing 142–3
continental grip 13
court etiquette 148–9
cross-court tactics 158, 159

D
Djokovic, Novak *9*
doubles:
    formations 164–5, 168
    poaching/intercepting 165
    returner 166
    returner's partner 167
    rules 147
    server's partner 165
    serving 165
    tactics 164–9
down the line tactics 158, 159
drive volley:
    forehand 126–31
    one-handed backhand 132–5
    two-handed backhand 136–9
drop shot:
    forehand 69
    one-handed backhand 45
drop volley:
    backhand 86–7
    forehand 74–5
Dushevina, Vera 167

E
eastern forehand grip 13
equipment 142–3
etiquette: on court 148–9

F
Federer, Roger *159*
first strikes: tactics 156–7
forced error 156
forehand:
    inside-in 159
    inside-out 159
forehand drive volley 126–31
    backswing 129
    contact point 130
    finish 131
    grip 127
    tracking ball 127
forehand drop shot 69
forehand drop volley 74–5
forehand half volley 80–1
forehand slice 62–8
    returning serve with 98
forehand smash 114–19
    contact point 117
    finish 119
    grip 115
    hand position 116
    wrist movement 118
forehand topspin 16–23
    backswing 20
    forward swing 21
    returning serve with 95
    tracking ball 19
forehand topspin lob 100–7
    backswing 104
    contact point 106
    finish 107
    forward swing 105
    grip 102
    tracking ball 103
forehand volley:
    drop 74–5
    high 70–3
        contact point 73
        grip 71
        tracking ball 72
    low 76–9
        contact point 79
        grip 77
        tracking ball 78
full western grip 14

G
games: scoring 144
grip 12–15

H

half volley:
    backhand 92–3
    forehand 80–1
hammer grip 13
hands: learning strokes with 10
heat: protection from 143
Henin, Justine *145*
Hepner, Jean 146

I

"I" formation 168
inside-in forehand 159
inside-out forehand 159

J

Jankovic, Jelena *141*

K

Kiefer, Nicolas *147*

L

Likhovtseva, Elena 167
line calling 148
lob:
    backhand topspin 108–13
    forehand topspin 100–7

M

matches: scoring 144
Mathieu, Paul-Henri *151*
mindset 162–3

N

Nadal, Rafael *12*, *156*
Nelson, Vicki 146

O

one-handed backhand drive volley
    132–5
    contact point 134
    finish 135
    grip 133
    tracking ball 133
one-handed backhand drop shot 45
one-handed slice backhand 38–44
    backswing 42
    contact point 43
    finish 44
    grip 40
    tracking ball 41
one-handed topspin backhand 32–7
    backswing 35
    contact point 36
    finish 37
    grip 15
    tracking ball 34

P

psychology 162–3

R

racket 143

spinning 148
    tracking ball with 11
racket bags 143
rally:
    rules 146
    tactics 160–1
Ratiwatana, Sanchai & Sonchat *169*
return of serve 94–9
returning:
    placement for 154
    stance and movement 170–1
    tactics 154–5
rituals 163
Roddick, Andy *143*, 147
rules 146–7

S

scoring 144–5
    point calling 145
semi-western grip 14
serve:
    deciding server 148
    returns of 94–9
    rules 146
    sidespin slice 46–53
    tactics 152–3
    topslice/topspin 54–61
    types 153
serve and volley 157
sets: scoring 144
shoes 143
sidespin slice serve 46–53
    contact point 51
    finish 53
    grip 48
slice 40, 48, 64
slice backhand:
    one-handed 38–44
        returning serve with 99
slice forehand 62–8
    backswing 66
    contact point 67
    finish 68
    grip 64
    returning serve with 98
    tracking ball 65
slice serve 153
    sidespin 46–53
smash:
    backhand 120–5
    forehand 114–19
spin: in volley 71, 77, 89
sportsmanship 149
striking the pose 11
strokes:
    finishing 11
    learning 10–11
sun: protection from 143

T

tactics 150–71
    cross court 158, 159
    doubles 164–9

down the line 158, 159
    first strikes 156–7
    rallying 160–1
    returning 154–5
    serving 152–3
    "Tandem" formation 168
tennis balls 142
timing 18
topspin forehand: lob 100–7
topslice 56
topslice serve 153
topslice/topspin serve 54–61
    contact point 59
    finish 61
    grip 56
topspin 18, 26, 33
topspin backhand:
    one-handed:
        grip 15
        returning serve with 96
    two-handed:
        grip 15
        returning serve with 97
topspin forehand: returning serve
    with 95
topspin lob:
    backhand 108–13
    forehand 100–7
tracking ball 11
two-handed backhand drive volley
    136–9
    contact point 138
    finish 139
    grip 137
    tracking ball 137
two-handed topspin backhand 24–31
    backswing 28
    contact point 30
    finish 31
    grip 15
    tracking ball 27

V

volley:
    backhand drop 86–7
    forehand drive 126–31
    forehand drop 74–5
    high forehand 70–3
    low backhand 88–91
    low forehand 76–9
    medium backhand 82–5
    two-handed backhand drive 136–9
Voltchkov, Vladimir 147

W

wheelchair tennis 147
Williams, Serena *142*
Williams, Venus 167
Wozniacki, Caroline 167

Special thanks to Kate Rudge and Simon Hardcastle for being such professional models.

Quarto would also like to thank the following for kindly supplying images for inclusion in this book:

Corbis
Getty Images
Shutterstock

All step-by-step and other images are the copyright of Quarto Publishing plc. Whilst every effort has been made to credit contributors, Quarto would like to apologize should there have been any omissions or errors, and would be pleased to make the appropriate correction for future editions of the book.

credits